The Savage Sacrament

The Savage Sacrament

A Theology of Marriage
After American Feminism

Eileen Zieget Silbermann

TWENTY-THIRD PUBLICATIONS
P.O. Box 180   Mystic, CT 06355

04-180

ISBN 0-89622-165-2

Library of Congress Catalog No. 82-50977

Edited by Amy Burman
Cover by William Baker
Book design by John G. van Bemmel

DEDICATION

for my husband in love
for our son, our daughters in hope
for our parents in memory

Preface

IN 1972, I BEGAN A FORMAL PROGRAM IN THE DISCIPLINE OF THEOLOGY at the Ecumenical Institute of Saint Mary's Seminary and University in Baltimore. The following January at a dinner party, I met the then newly ordained Bishop James Rausch, who remarked to me over coffee, "If you ever write anything in theology, do something on the theology of marriage. We need it."

My response then was that there cannot be a cohesive theology of marriage until the church recognizes the importance of women, their true equality, their significant contributions to the world, their basic human needs, and their legitimate concerns. That is a long list. Theology has been and still is a patrilinear system; it neither knows nor cares about the multiplicity of women's thoughts or feelings or desires.

The bishop and I agreed that my answer was a harsh indictment against a church we both loved deeply; I do not recall that there was any argument about its credibility.

In retrospect, that conversation was a kind of conversion experience. I had never considered myself a feminist. At a meeting of the Governor's Commission on the Status of Women in the State of Maryland, I had once listened in horror to someone recounting the evils of showing mothers in rocking chairs in first and second grade readers. I had rocked three babies in such a creaky relic and loved every minute of it!

My academic appointment then, and now, was in the Department of Philosophy at Essex Community College in Baltimore County. As an adjunct to that position, I also directed for a time an outreach program designed to encourage women to return to college, or to commence a program of study. The venture has enjoyed a more than modest success in the capable hands of Shirley Saxton, and all of us who ever worked in it have had some extravagant rewards.

As a result of this involvement, the last decade has provided ample opportunities for me to listen to literally hundreds of women in classrooms and supermarkets, in meeting rooms, and over the phone in the middle of the night. I have read their term papers and book reports, their personality profiles, their autobiographies, and their stories.

Many were women caught in a time of radical change; the old female role models were not adequate for them, and yet they were chary of the new "liberated" model. Almost all of these women were or had been married, and often enough described themselves as happy. I was not always certain that one state had anything much to do with the other. Most came to the college and to the program for the simple reason that they wanted a little more from life and from marriage. I found a beautiful felicity in their womanliness. I did not find them to be malcontents, malingerers, bitches, hags, bitter, or angry women.

To relate to their needs more effectively, I began to read about women by women, and I learned how to define feminism. I read De Beauvoir, Morgan, Ruether, Daly, Friedan, Dinnerstein, Janeway, and Millet; and I read them concurrently with Rahner, Lonergan, Tillich, Barth, Haring, Kung, Bonhoeffer and Jeremias. I wondered, remembering the new bishop's request, if there was any way to put them together.

What would happen to theology after American feminism?

I read about marriage and its rich and varied history. The rude and ruthless practices of capture in primitive marriages, the singular symbols and customs of various African tribes fascinated me, as did the superstitions that surrounded sex and marriage in ancient Ireland. Fascination turned into horror as I went over the accounts of the torture of chastity belts, the crippling of Chinese footbinding, suttee, witch hunts, clitoridectomies, and the cold denigration of women by men who were revered as brilliant and holy and powerful. They certainly were powerful.

I read Freud and Augustine, *Gaudium et Spes* and *Open Marriage*, and a great deal of the process philosophy of Alfred North Whitehead. I reread *Humanae Vitae*, every word.

In 1975, several months were spent on a study that involved the wives of the permanent deacons in the Archdiocese of Baltimore. This work was then expanded to a more extensive survey based on studies done by Virginia Heffernan in the Washington Archdiocese. Both investigations were called "Women in the Pew."

I became curious about how Catholic women viewed sacramental marriage as different from a good or satisfying or successful marriage that had been formalized in some city hall. Those women I asked generally theologized about marriage by way of customs and canons and encyclical letters they had never read in their entirety. This means, I think, that most women do not see a significant difference at all, and so for them there is no meaningful understanding of the theology of marriage. Marriage was fragmented, dislocated, or uncertain once theology was introduced into the field of concentration. Someone asked me if I thought women's theology of marriage was bankrupt; I am not sure that it even existed.

We know that only a handful of the Hebrews followed Moses out of the bondage of Egyptian slavery into the desert, past Sinai, and on into the Promised Land. Many of those who began with a vision of faith had second thoughts about the process and its wisdom.

Today only a handful of Christian women call themselves feminists, and mean a varied intensity in that definition. Exodus tells us unequivocally that "the whole community of the sons of Israel began to complain against Moses and Aaron in the wilderness . . ." (Exodus: 16:2). There is no such generalization possible for the whole community of the daughters of today's feminism.

Therefore, I make no sweeping claim to speak for all Catholic women, or for all feminists. I live and work in Baltimore, and most of the women whose thoughts or experiences appear or are recounted in these pages make their homes in the same metropolitan area.

Perhaps women of the rural communities of the Midwest and the South, women trying to make a home amid the squalor of the industrial wasteland, the inhabitants of the larger and more cosmopolitan cities of our nation may find other and clearer evaluations of what "feminist women" say about marriage. If they do, I trust that they will articulate their findings.

This book was written in hope. I think that hope is never something passive, not redemptive hope anyway. Erich Fromm says that hope is like a "crouched tiger." He goes on to point out that there is "no sense in hoping for that which already exists or for that which cannot be." There is no real fusion that already exists between the feminist writers and the theologians, but I will not believe that none can be brought about.

What follows is a coming together in my own mind of all the reading and all the interviews, a coalescence of my own lived experience of marriage, and my observant listening to others.

The "tigress," having decided the moment for jumping has come, is about to do just that.

My gratitude goes out to all those hundreds of women who shared with me so much of their own lives. I trust that I have been faithful to their revelations.

More than a mention of thanks must go to Marie Sloane Tillman. If I could design the perfect friend, she would be Marie, who listened endlessly, encouraged, praised, and corrected. Marie and James Tillman came as close as any couple I have been privileged to know to the wholesome realization of what Christian marriage is all about. I write this past tense in pain. Jim Tillman died February 12, 1982. The savage aspects of that marriage have just begun.

My own life has been touched by the richness of many special and strong women. Over many, many years Jane Davis Carduff, Deborah Barcus Jones, Carmen Croke McFarland, Dorothy Pula Strohecker and Eleanor Hughes John have wept and rejoiced with me. I thank them for the decades of devotion, and for the beautiful examples of their marriages. Indeed, for me, they have made a difference.

I married Joseph Michael Silbermann on June 13, 1953. We have a son, Neil, and two daughters, Anne and Clare. In our wedding bands Joe had engraved a quotation from Dante, "In His Will is Our Peace." We still believe that truth.

Contents

Introduction

CHRISTIAN THEOLOGIANS — CHRISTIAN FEMINISTS. WHAT WOULD THEY speak to one another in dialogue? And if there is no present dialogue, where can a beginning be found for an exploration of the attitudes of each group when they address the role of women expected in Christian marriage?

At the dawn of revelation, God gave his world, a Paradise, to man and to woman. Genesis 2:18 reveals that Yahweh said: "It is not good that man should be alone." But the man and woman abandoned God and in the process lost the purity of their original relationship to each other. The tone of the language shifts. In Genesis 3:16 Yahweh rebukes the woman: "Your yearning shall be for your husband, yet he will lord it over you." So as punishment, women have been submissive to their husbands and given birth to their children in pain these many centuries after the fall, and after the redemption too. Abraham prayed to God, Jeremiah argued with him, Job confronted the divine pleasure, but for women there has been no answer, no retort, no dialogue.

An arbitrary opening of the Book of Proverbs yielded this saying: "It is better to live in a desert land than with a contentious and fretful woman" (Proverbs 21:19). This is hardly an isolated idea for the writers of the Wisdom literature. There is no written record of the response of the women living at that time, but today's feminist, who would not contradict the wisdom, does counter with an observation. Dorothy Samuel says:

> That a man could not be a fully functioning human being nor a truly happy and contented marriage partner when frustrated in the work for which he cared has long been a preachment to women, to wives. Only now are we beginning to realize that many of the discontented and unhappy wives of the past were formed by the constant frustration of their own talents and ambitions.

This may be a beginning of dialogue.

Feminists who know anything about sacred scripture are certain that they will find material for argumentation in the writings of Saint Paul. In his letter to Titus, for example, Paul offered some helpful advice about the role of the wife in Christian marriage. "They are to be sensible and chaste, and . . . work in their homes, and be gentle, and do as their husbands tell them, so that the message of God is never disgraced" (Titus 2:5).

Christian women are not anxious to disgrace God's message, but they may want to dialogue from the perspective of Jean Baker Miller, M.D., who says this about the subordination of women:

> Dominant groups usually define one or more acceptable roles for the subordinate. Acceptable roles typically involve providing services that no dominant group wants to perform for itself. It follows that subordinates are described in terms of, and encouraged to develop, personal psychological characteristics that are pleasing to the dominant group . . . submissiveness, passivity, docility, dependency, lack of initiative, inability to act, to decide, to think, and the like. . . .

If a reader were to peruse Stephen B. Clark's 1980 publication of *Man and Woman in Christ*, an examination of the roles of men and women in the light of scripture and the social sciences, she would find this summary: "All Christians saw a clear teaching in scripture, unambiguously supported in the Fathers, and they were committed to a Christian approach to family life, even when they might not live out that commitment well." The reader would also find references to the 1920 encyclical letter of Pius XI, *Casti Connubii*, which read: "Physiological emancipation would free women at will from wifely and maternal responsibilities, and this . . . is not emancipation but an abominable crime."

It is one thing to react to the vilification of women by men like Schopenhauer or Nietzsche; after all, they do not have the full weight of tradition behind them. It is quite another to tackle phrases like "abominable crime" when they come from a papal pen. Feminist writers, free of deferential constraint, have expressed an opposite view. Adrienne Rich writes:

> The experience of maternity and the experience of sexuality have been channeled to serve male interests. Patriarchy would seem to require, not only that women shall assume the major burden of pain and self-denial for the furtherance of the species, that a majority of that species — women — shall remain essentially unquestioning and unenlightened.

Try the angle of canon law. A feminist who picked up Bernard Siegle's commentary on the Code of Canon Law on marriage, would inevitably read in his introduction the elegant theological statement:

> The Savior of men and Spouse of the Church comes into the lives of married Christians through the sacrament of matrimony. He abides with them thereafter so that just as He loved the Church and handed Himself over on her behalf, the spouses may love each other with perpetual fidelity through mutual self-giving.

The canonist might wander down the aisle to the sociology section of the bookstore and find a tougher observation of marriage by Terry Davidson, who writes:

> Conjugal crime is estimated by law enforcement officials to be a phenomenon few people are willing to discuss, touching perhaps 50 percent of American marriages and seriously threatening the safety of a significant percentage of women and their children on a nightmarishly recurring basis.

Davidson doesn't say, but certainly some of those battered wives must wear gold bands blessed in a sacramental ceremony.

An obvious source of information on the current status of the theology of marriage is the 1968 encyclical letter of Pope Paul VI, *Humanae Vitae,* which deals with the regulation of human birth. The document was preceded by dialogue with a commission of experts that included some laity along with the expected episcopal and theological membership. But Paul chose to dismiss the informed opinion of the group, and stood firm on his, and his venerable predecessors', position on the issues of artificial contraception and birth control. He also advised married couples:

> Do not therefore, let yourselves be led astray by the temptations, difficulties and trials that arise along the way. Do not be afraid, when necessary, to go against the tide of thought and opinion of a world ruled by paganized standards of behavior. Saint Paul warns us: "Do not accommodate yourselves to the customs of the age you live in. . . ."

The response, and a caveat, might come from *Reinventing Womanhood* by Carolyn Heilbrun:

> Marriage can be preserved only if we allow family structure to change. Institutions that cannot adapt will not survive. That is the lesson conservatives stubbornly refuse to learn, perhaps because admitting its truth fatally weakens the logic of their position.

There are no qualms in the admission that these are a skimpy and haphazard group of quotations. I had no special method lurking behind their selection. There is, however, a definite purpose in their presentation here. The dialogue is intended to illustrate, I wish I could say headline, the often extreme polarity of the two positions. While it should be expected that a wide range of expression will always exist among commentators on any controversial issue, be they theologians or feminists or anyone else, I needed to show immediately that the square-off is definitely real.

If this divisiveness is pervasive, where does it leave women who are serious about their faith and their feminism? Can they have both?

One wonders if there is any hope of a merger, a reconciliation, and the question must be asked: Have the social currents of the modern world moved Christian feminists beyond the reach and understanding of a truly faithful theology of marriage?

And where does the divisiveness leave the Church? Is there no hope that the ancient institution will even listen to its modern daughters who want more than moral indifference and intellectual exercises from that which they, too, call Holy Mother?

Chapter One

Marriage:
The Savage Sacrament

Then the Lord said, "Go outside and stand on the mountain before the Lord; the Lord will be passing by." A strong and heavy wind was rending the mountains and crushing rocks before the Lord—but the Lord was not in the wind. After the wind there was an earthquake. After the earthquake there was fire—but the Lord was not in the fire. After the fire there was a tiny whispering sound. When he heard this, Elijah hid his face in his cloak and went and stood at the entrance of the cave.

1 Kings 19:11-13

IN 1980, AMERICA CELEBRATED THE YEAR OF THE FAMILY. FOR THE most part, family in this culture still means marriage, and marriage for most Catholics means a sacramental union. Sacraments are the sacred, the grace-giving signs studied by theology; theology, even in a modern and secular world, is still about the encounter between God and human persons.

The sacrament that unites a man and a woman in Christian marriage is the concern of this investigation. Exactly half of the human persons who meet the God of Love in this sacrament are women. Inquiries about the relationship between theology and feminism have never been of significant interest to either feminists or theologians. Patriarchal religion has traditionally regarded women as the "second sex," a malignant image that endures even as Christian times approach the twenty-first century. Feminists, generally outraged by the dismal history of the treatment of women by theology, have concluded that their struggle for freedom, equality, and personhood might be worked out with little reference to a church that will allow them no power and only a marginal voice. Theologians too often have retreated into custom, tradition, the teachings of the Fathers and the scriptures; their hands are folded righteously because the last truth has already been delivered.

There is little wisdom in maintaining this stance, and formidable consequences for persisting in it. The most obvious reason is that mutual indifference will continue to impoverish both women and the church.

The voice of woman in theology is no longer mute. In October of 1979 the soft, deferential voice of one woman pleaded with Pope John Paul II, asking only that he listen to the voices of women who have felt betrayed by the church of their deeply experienced spiritual needs. It was a quiet and, indeed, a simple petition, and then Sister Theresa Kane, R.S.M., knelt in stunned silence in the Catholic University of America to receive the pontiff's blessing.

Her courageous action was not solidly affirmed even by the religious women she represented. (Women have been trained to beg delicately.) Still, there is a growing commitment to the necessity for women to tell of their own needs and hopes, to utter their own visions and insights. Feminists are not complacent, and they cannot be if they are ever to do a theology that is more than an insipid chronicle.

Women know about marriage; the contract/covenant/sacrament is an intimate part of their lives. They play at being married when they are little girls, they dream of being married when they are adolescents, they pray for marriage as young women, and finally, as adults, most of them experience it. For better or worse.

One thing women have not done is talk about marriage in relation to theology, which is a process of interpreting life in the light of faith. Until recent times, few women have been trained and degreed in theology, and those who were competent in the discipline tended to be religious women who, understandably, had other concerns.

This work is an attempt to correct the lack of dialogue between women and theologians. It is not a history. It is a reading of contemporary women, American women, a new breed perhaps, women who may or may not identify themselves as feminists, but who do proclaim that freedom and dignity for their sex should exist in all areas of human life.

Some of the women whose thoughts and experiences are articulated in these pages are degreed in theology. Included are professional women who bring their expertise in such varied fields as sociology, psychology, anthropology, literature, history (herstory), medicine, and law to illuminate the situation of modern women in society and in the church. Some women are radical feminists, some women are active in a career, and others have no major commitments outside the home.

Some women are young brides, some are great-grandmothers. Some women wear tailored suits and sit in executive offices, some push strollers around in the ghetto, some scrub the famed marble steps of East Baltimore. They are Catholic women whose experience of marriage is sacramental.

The theologians are also contemporary, and their work is of the post-Vatican II era of the Roman Catholic tradition. Not all are Americans because theology is written in a transcultural vein. The books I picked up for reference are on the shelves of most Catholic bookstores. I did not do much poking around in the archives of seminary and university libraries. I was interested in what a woman might find available to read if she developed an interest in the theology of marriage.

If any justification for this dialogue is needed, there is the simple offering that whatever has been taught or written on the theology of marriage, has been, with few and very recent exceptions, taught and written by men. The vast majority of these men have been celibate. The bulk of what they wrote into their theology and canon law and norms of morality was written without the experience and consultation of women, an idiocy that is only understandable in light of an ideology that viewed women as inherently defective, unclean, inferior, and occasions of sin.

The timing for such a dialogue may not be fortuitous. Americans are living in a society marked by economic depression, ecological concern, an unsettling and unstable transformation of familial values and gender roles, a time of confusion and deepening malaise. It is a time, described by Alvin Toffler in *The Third Wave*, when "value systems splinter and crash, while the lifeboats of family, church and state are hurled madly about."

Centuries of tradition are under attack as women begin to address a church, itself tormented by a conflict of ideals. There are feminists who are scholars, but theirs is a scholarship turned to passion. "Women's studies do not pretend to an ethical neutrality," Rosemary Ruether insists. "Neutrality hides a commitment to the status quo."

Feminists seem to understand in a profound way that women need to examine and then speak from their own experience, and that they are "no longer content to feel, judge and act exclusively according to the modes and standards deemed appropriate in a patriarchal cultural tradition." Attempting to define a definitive feminist position, Carolyn Heilbrun goes on to say: "Womanhood can be what we say it is, not what they have always said it was."

The current situation of American women is undergoing a massive critique, and women's role in marriage and the family is an arrangement in which the crisis is acute. Women are walking away from marriage in unprecedented numbers. The accumulated years of frustration, occasioned by the confines of their lives, have led to a choice that reflects desperation as well as a vital determination to begin their lives over again.

They are walking away from the church, too, or at least ceasing their active involvement in church organizations. It is no longer enough for theology to try to understand the special oppression that women feel, to appreciate that blind submission and personal authenticity are not always compatible. Theology must demonstrate an active involvement and sincere investment in changing the existing reality in which this oppression takes its form.

Women, silent and enduring for centuries, have ripped off the gag and ignored the command of silence attributed to Saint Paul. While still denied any official vehicle of audience by the dominant authorities of their church, women in America and elsewhere now have access to the professions as well as the public forum, and they speak with their own authority. The feminist movement with its standard cry, "Sisterhood is powerful!" has provided a strong support system. We have not really tested how powerful sisterhood might be.

Some Christian feminists have abandoned their religious affiliations because they perceive the institutional church as sexist and therefore irrelevant to women. Others, recognizing this demonic aspect of the church's structures, nevertheless struggle to believe that they can find some strains of hope that its constraints and negative, life-destroying elements will somehow be transformed. In either case the stakes are high.

The church is a powerful cultural institution, and may indeed elect to crush the potential and creativity of its daughters, even though that decision may warp and diminish its own life. It has had hundreds of years of practice. When it follows the norms of the Second Vatican Council, the church staunchly defends and focuses its concern on the values of human dignity and personal freedom. The Council Fathers declared: "Persons and societies thirst for a full and free life worthy of man—one in which they can subject to their own welfare all that the modern world can offer them so abundantly."

Well, women thirst, too. And now women, to borrow a phrase from Bonhoeffer, have truly come of age.

The naming of the year 1980 as a celebration of the particular kind of commitment we call family may indeed have arisen from an anxiety that there is precious little to celebrate. Families, including Catholic families, are in trouble in America. Statistics show an increasing proportion in the number of incomplete homes. The traditional or conventional family, a lifestyle that has come to be known as the nuclear family, consisting of the bread-winner father, the housewife mother, and their children, is now a national minority group. Roughly 7 percent of the nation's households actually conform to this structure. Divorce, separation, desertion, and all the assorted varieties of non-marriage are no longer rare occurrences in American life, and the statistics scream rather than suggest a progressive disintegration of marriage and the family.

Married couples do not always demand and expect sexual fidelity of each other; today the promise of lifetime fidelity or commitment is anticipated more as casual phraseology than as solemn vow. There are accounts of married couples who swap partners for the evening or the weekend, and monogamy, while ostensibly an ideal, is frequently practiced as serial or sequential monogamy.

The svelte popular magazines headline the information that adultery may ultimately enhance the quality of the existing marriage. It is all part of the credentials race for the superlative payoff of the "open marriage." Nena and George O'Neill emphasize that fidelity in the "closed marriage" is in reality a measure of *"limited love, diminished growth and conditional trust."* Sexual fidelity is a false god, they say.

Parenthood is completely disavowed by some couples, either by an explicit premarital agreement or sterilization, or, implicitly, by the eternal postponement of procreation. Other couples, concerned about the limitations of responsible parenthood, are curtailing the number of children by whatever means their conscience, medical science, or the law permits.

About one-third of all abortions in the nation are performed on married women; these statistics are listed in six figures.

The data from the 1980 census reveal that seven years is the average length of the American marriage. In some states the constantly accelerating divorce rate means that every other marriage is terminated by the courts. Second marriages do not seem to fare much better, since 40 percent of these unions also end in divorce. There is no solid evidence to suggest that the results of the next census will improve these staggering figures.

The census data are national and include all marriages. Saving mystery that sacramental marriage is declared to be, the human reality does not appear to exclude it from the dreary statistics nor exempt it from disturbance. The thousands of annulments applied for and granted in recent years by overworked tribunal officials bear this out.

No one will easily deny that the bare mathematical listings even begin to catalogue the anguish, fear, and confusion, indeed the wreckage, of those unions that somehow remain intact for one reason or another, but fail nonetheless because they are barren and sterile. As one woman, quite aware that marriage was created to ensure the appropriate conditions for the optimum growth of human love and personal fulfillment, said: "It is not that my marriage is so bad; it is just empty."

For many women, marriage is a savage sacrament.

"Savage" is a strong word, a problematic word. It means fierce, ferocious, cruel. Synonyms are "barbarous" and "uncivilized." To speak of savagery in sacramental marriage borders on the blasphemous.

That beautiful young couple slipping golden rings over smooth-skinned fingers, smiling radiantly after the blessing, are full of hope and joyous anticipation. Soon they will move to the little house with the white picket fence, and plant a tree the day their first child is born. Neighbors will watch them dutifully attend the 10:30 Mass every Sunday, and they can be counted on to help with the carnival. They will teach their children the Our Father and grace before meals; they will make weekend retreats and plan the Advent customs; they will grow old together in peace before the Lord. How is marriage savage?

Is this glowing image truly nothing more than a wish, a dream, a fantasy, an ideal? Is living happily ever after only a childish, fairytale notion? Are American Catholics so seduced by the romantic notion of love in ways that preclude even the possibility of a thoughtful reflection that could intervene to give a hypothetical character to some marvelous absolute?

What is savage for women in Christian marriage? Women answered:

"Savage is changing your name."

"Savage is faking an orgasm, and he does not even realize it."

"Savage is having to entertain his boss and his clients at the expense of spending time with your friends."

"Savage is knowing that you will never come up to the standards of his parents."

"Savage is knowing that he is having an affair."

"Savage is being alone in the suburbs."

"Savage is coming home from work later than he does and having to do all the household chores."

"Savage is getting pregnant, receiving those flowery congratulations, and smiling to hide your absolute terror."

"Savage is wanting your husband with you in the delivery room, and he is afraid — or playing golf."

"Savage is putting the fourth child into the one bedroom."

"Savage is eating peanut butter and jelly sandwiches, taking care of sick kids, waiting for his call from San Francisco, and all he can talk about is how great the lobster thermidor was at Fisherman's Wharf."

"Savage is being struck, and lying about it to hospital attendants. It is wearing dark glasses and praying no one will ask questions."

"Savage is having no support at all when you only want to go back to school or join a literary group."

"Savage is being ill, but getting up to fix dinner and iron his shirt anyway."

"Savage is having six pregnancies in eight years and feeling guilty about taking the pill."

"Savage is being threatened with divorce, and knowing that you have no job skills but three children to support."

"Savage is being excluded from church groups after you are divorced, and facing years of stark loneliness when your sexual needs are still strong."

"Savage is having a retarded child, and being blamed for his condition."

"Savage is building up a practice, he's transferred, and the years of work are down the drain."

"Savage is knowing that grey hair makes him look distinguished, while it only means you are old."

"Savage is having to ask for money."

"Savage is having nothing to say to each other."

The list, of course, is endless. It is uneven in significance. Some of the definitions may reveal a selfishness, a petty superficiality. It would take volumes of analytical work to lay bare the life stories that produced them.

The new sense of Christian sisterhood, Christian feminism, listens to the voices of women who cry out that much of this savagery does not have to be. It is not redemptive. It is not revelatory of the presence of God in the lives of Christian women.

The tragedy that many women experience in their marriages does not provoke the conclusion that the marital relationship is fundamentally pernicious and destructive. The drama and the dream of conjugal love is as old as human life. There are magnificent marriages. What women say is that the church needs to be more sensitive to those that are not.

Gregory Baum reminds Christians that they must listen to the truth wherever, and by whom, it is uttered if they are to be faithful to the divine word, once and for all revealed in Christ.

The Christian Church must listen to what this Word, present in woman's historical experience, is saying to it now. The normative apostolic witness to Christ enables the Church to discern in the chorus of voices that surround it the divine message addressed to it. Thanks to this process, in which the whole community is involved, which is tested by scripture, exposed to dialogue and even conflict, and ultimately acknowledged by the ecclesiastical authorities, the Church is able to proclaim the Word of God, faithful to the Apostolic norm, as the Good News for the present.

Theologian Monika Hellwig, recognizing that the theology of marriage has had a long and difficult chronology, notes that

it took twelve centuries of Christian history for our tradition to formulate a theology of marriage as a sacrament and even then we had to go on waiting to the present century for theologians to ask more of the really fundamental questions about it.

One of those fundamental questions must be relational to women and their value judgments on how sacramental marriage affects their lives, their growing development as persons, and finally, their perfection as Christians.

Marriage as it has been expounded by the soaring spirituality of the theologians, and marriage as it is lived out, do not always seem to be the same. If an earlier theology was written without a significant interest in how women are affected by its doctrine and patriarchal canon law, then the workableness of that theology and that law will be altered in a serious way as women seize their own identity within the world and the church.

Christianity cannot, after all, be totally divorced from reality.

CHAPTER TWO

Inherited "Official" Views of Marriage

You are the children of saints, and cannot be joined together like the heathen."

Tobit 8:5

IN "SEXUAL MORALITY: A CATHOLIC PERSPECTIVE," PHILIP S. KEANE, S.S., points out that the church does not yet possess an extensive theology of marriage, and he affirms that the development of one is "the greatest single task for the Church to undertake."

Essentially, Keane is correct. A check of the card catalogs of several Catholic colleges and universities did not yield a substantial bibliography on the theology of marriage. Edward Schillebeeckx's monumental work, *Marriage: Human Reality and Saving Mystery*, stands in an almost isolated splendor. After reading this (it had to be special ordered), the researcher must fumble and ferret through relatively brief treatments by the dogmatic theologians who have contentedly reiterated the major conclusions of the canonists and moral philosopher-theologians.

This is not to say that there are not many books on marriage; there are quite a few. Even a cursory evaluation of most theological writings shows that they emanate either from an ethical point of view or the social problem perspective. Canon lawyers write about marriage from the juridical perspective.

Keane himself discusses the issues of pre-marital sex, extramarital activities, the sexual communion of the couple during marriage, the morality of contraceptives, and the sterilization procedures, abortion, artificial insemination, divorce, annulment, and remarriage.

Canonists such as Stephen Kelleher, William Bassett, and John Finnegan detail the refinement of church law and the problems of tribunal practice. Bernard Siegle incorporates recent canonical jurisprudence with the theologically maturing spirit of the post-Vatican II years, but he is first and foremost a canonist.

The social problem perspective of marriage is treated by authors such as Clayton Barbeau, Eugene Kennedy, Jack Dominian, Evelyn and James Whitehead, and Andrew Greeley. James Burtchaell, of the Theology Department of the University of Notre Dame, has edited a fine collection of essays by Catholic laymen, a work similar to one done by Michael Novak in the mid-sixties. All of these writings are extremely valuable.

There is probably no single answer to the question of what marriage, any marriage, means. It is an ancient institution, although diverse and variegated.

Anthropologists, systematically collecting evidence from primitive societies, found that marriage as a secular reality was firmly established when recorded history began a few thousand years ago, long before the advent of Israel. As a human institution, it has been regarded as the basic building block of society, a human substratum, a viable system. The association of a man and woman formed the family unit in which the partners found some sort of personal fulfillment.

Some kind of family structure has existed in all known human societies, although familial life is not found in every segment or class of all stratified, state societies. Family was an ideal that all classes and most individuals attained when they could. The history of the family has led contemporary theologians to recognize that the church does not own marriage; it was and is given to the human race.

At the same time, the theologians believe that the revelation of both the Old and New Testaments has cast a special light upon the human couple. "The starting point of the world, as God sees it," Marc Oraison says succinctly, "is said to be this relation of the couple, of man and woman." The relationship of marriage has served as the principal paradigm for understanding how men and women should be related in human affairs.

Oraison goes on to affirm the common teaching that the main topic of revelation is that of the dramatic split between God and man as described in Genesis, and the ensuing reconciliation that came about in the alliance or covenant that God made with man for his eternal salvation. The allegory most capable of expressing this covenantal love, this great mystery, is the human couple united in conjugal love. Genesis makes it clear that this prime analog is privileged because it reveals a man and a woman as the image of God.

The theme of God as the infinitely tender, always faithful and loving bridegroom, and Israel as the faithless and defective bride, runs through Hosea, Isaias, Ezechiel, and the Song of Songs. It peaks in the letters of Saint Paul where he elevates marriage to the symbol of Christ's great love for his church. "Husbands should love their wives just as Christ loved the Church and sacrificed himself for her to make her holy" (Ephesians 5:25).

Bernard Haring speaks of marriage as sacrament as the prototype of the covenant between God and humankind, and between Christ and the church. "The readiness to forgive, to heal, to help, to bear the burdens of each other, and gently to offer encouragement and correction, are an essential part of Christian Matrimony that reflects the convenant of God with mankind."

What seems to be unique to this aspect of biblical revelation is precisely the linkage between a human person's understanding of God and her understanding of marriage and the mystery of human love. The sacrament reveals dimensions of God previously unknown. Part of the medium by which God tells womankind something about himself is to be found in the human response to love that is equated in the intense and profoundly intimate relationship of Christian marriage. It is dialectical. In revelation God takes this human situation and affirms that it is holy, and this means that marriage has an important significance for woman's active approach to God, and for her ability to interpret and celebrate this human experience in the light of faith. Consideration of a theology of marriage should yield conclusions that are consequential to the total life of any woman, both in belief and practice.

The single and essential condition for Christian marriage in the thought of Saint Paul is that it should be "in the Lord." Rosemary Haughton, in her treatment of the sublime symbolism of Christian marriage, sees the conjugal union as integrated into the full flowering of the new life that is the Christian experience. Christian marriage is more than a social arrangement or institution; its character surpasses a merely legislative way of regulating sex. Christian marriage is indeed a great mystery, the very mystery of redemption. "In the Lord, then, human marriage finds its eternal and proper reality, in the bridal relationship of God with his people."

In the same vein, Karl Rahner calls marriage a holy adventure, a part of the mystery of God. (Mystery is a word the theologians employ repetitively.) It is an experience that partakes of the divine, involving the whole woman and her destiny. It is God who is the fulfillment of the infinite promise of love; it is God who is the guardian of the dignity of the person who lovingly trusts herself to another; it is God who is true forgiveness and holy fidelity; it is God who understands the unfathomable depth in grace of the other human being. All of this is true, Rahner says homiletically, because God is love itself, and therefore the source of all other loves.

The human couple must always be open to God, to his love, his faithfulness, and forgiveness. A marriage that lacks this openness and vision of faith is a blind marriage, and may, he warns, become a dangerous experience for the partners.

But whoever truly loves knows what love is. And only those who have known it can understand that God Himself is love. For what can we hope to know if we have no notion of who He is, the incomprehensible, the holy mystery which en-

folds us and in which we find in all our doing, our daily, lifelong experience of the painful inexpressibility of love.

In *Foundations of Christian Faith,* Rahner deemphasizes the
easy impression that the similarity between Christ and the church
in one instance, and the union of man and woman in marriage in
the other, lies in the notion that the husband represents Christ
while the wife represents the church. (By extension, the husband
might be considered to represent God, and the wife, faithless Israel,
an analogy many women find distasteful.) Rahner thinks that the
central assertion of the text from Ephesians 5:29-33 is that it is the
unity of the love itself that constitutes the parallel between Christ-
church and marriage. This union in love "unites the persons themselves in their final and definitive validity" hidden under the veil of
faith and hope.

The underlying meaning and experience of marriage has been
given a different emphasis at various times in the long history of the
church, and human societies as well. Not always listed among the
several sacraments, marriage at one time was regarded simply as a
perfectly natural event that was blessed liturgically by a priest or
bishop who had come to congratulate the new family and celebrate
the marriage feast. In another era, marriage was considered as a
legal and social institution, a contract, a procreative bond.

Today, many see the model of marriage as an authentic inter-
personal relationship based on a promise that has the power to
summon the couple to a new experience, a new mode of being.
Marriage and its rituals do not differ from the other sacraments
whose emphasis has shifted over the centuries, in response to various cultures, societies, or essential human needs.

Marriage has served many human purposes, but its abiding
human motive is the fact that every individual finds herself lonely
and incomplete. Married love is the attempt to alleviate or assuage
that loneliness. The author of Genesis knew this well, "It is not
good for man to be alone. . . ." As married love is cultivated, it expands and ultimately knows no boundaries. The loneliness and in-
completeness of the individual are lost when the ecstacy of married
love is brought to the understanding and knowledge of God.

Edward Schillebeeckx, in his impressive study of marriage in
both Old and New Testaments, as well as marriage in the history of

the church, states that the distinctive quality of Christian marriage is found in its reality that is secular in origin, but which has acquired a deeper meaning in the order of salvation. Salvation vivifies life, and therefore points to something higher. In human marriage the symbol is real, and its reality is symbolic. He writes: "The definitive surrender to another person, without any foreknowledge of what may happen in the future is the human manifestation of man's definitive surrender to the other being, God."

The grace of matrimony is the grace of Christ. "Husbands and wives, love one another as Christ loved the Church and gave himself up for her" (Ephesians 5:25). Thomas N. Hart, who teaches theology and also does marriage counseling, does an exegesis on this text.

> Now we can better understand what that injunction means, what kind of love it is that Christian marriage is intended to incarnate. It is self-giving love, bringing the other to wholeness and holiness. It is faithful love, abiding and there to be relied upon even when all rightful claim has been forfeited. This is a weighty charge, yet our text unmistakably brings marriage right into line with Christ's way of loving his Church.

Another American theologian, Daniel Di Domizio, uses a similar terminology to describe sexuality in marriage as a sacramental event, and adds a touch of psychological jargon and a hint of process philosophy. He says:

> The prophets speak of the marriage between God and Israel as everlasting and yet as an on-again, off-again experience, at least on the part of Israel. The Song of Songs beautifully describes the approach withdrawal dynamic of the two lovers. The New Testament speaks of the consummation of the marriage between Christ and his Church in the blood of the Cross; yet St. Paul also alludes to the fidelity of the Church as spouse amid the tensions of everyday life. The point is that, as all married persons know so well, the sacrament of marriage is happening throughout the relationship, not just on the wedding day.

James Burtchaell observes that the formality of pledging has always been a potent strategy for bringing about an emergence from self-centeredness into love. Marriage has the fundamental sacramental value of securing the process of a constant giving of self, and makes the discovery of genuine personhood possible and authentic. Jesus seemed to invite his followers to a dynamic marital commitment that "was an unremitting promise of fidelity, free of conditions on which one could and might withdraw, and it was the ground for a more demanding love and a more accurate trust."

He goes on to affirm that the vows of sacramental marriage are as awesome a pledge as one person can give another: the pledge unto death. "Between man and wife it is as between disciple and Jesus: one will be loved, one can claim to be loved, whatever one's faults. One need not be anxious whether one will continue to be cherished. One is literally forgiven before the fall."

Indeed Saint Paul was correct, this is a great mystery.

In a lyrical way the language and glowing ideals of the theologians express the hopes, dreams, and desires of most couples as they prepare for sacramental marriage. The bride and groom envision a loving, living union, a lifetime of delight in discovering the other. They look forward to a reciprocity between two individuals who are free to grow as persons, constantly changing as men and women whose ultimate mystery can never be exhausted. Marriage should be the greatest joy given to women on this earth.

But somehow, something seems to be lost in the translation. When the lyrical, the poetic language is taken down to the bare bones, some of the savage in the sacrament begins to appear. Only the hopelessly romantic expect the flawless, perfect love. But it is also true that the fruitful flowering of human love, intended by the creator and by him made holy, cannot be yielded by decadent and barren roots.

"Why," Karen Horney asks, "are good marriages so rare — marriages that do not stifle the developmental potential of the partners, marriages in which undercurrents of tension do not reverberate in the home or in which they are so intense they have brought about a benevolent indifference?" Even the best of marriages may harbor some fragile element, and stress can shatter so easily. The failed marriage, like a virus, can infect other relationships and even subsequent generations. It certainly affects the church.

William W. Bassett, writing in 1968 when he was an Assistant Professor of Canon Law at the Catholic University of America, says that perhaps as many as a million adults a year do not participate in the sacramental life of the church because they cannot or will not sustain a permanent marriage.

Marriages fail with increasing frequency, but the Church is able to help but a few of the millions of those who fail with them. To those who suffer in isolation and loneliness, to those who are abandoned or who live in the snakepits of hostility, it is not enough to appeal to the consistence of tribunal procedure or even, anymore, to the authority of the Church's law. This law and its authority can no longer help preserve the holiness of marriage for the vast majority of mankind.

Jesus also called us to live in peace.

On an elementary level, if such a complex human/legal/social/religious institution can ever be reduced to such a dimension, the churchmen tell us that God created men and women with distinct yet complementary natures. Sexuality was given by God for the purpose of procreation and the sustenance of new life, and for the perfection and support of the individual partners.

The natural, secular institution of marriage was made a sacrament by Christ, and so now is a privileged instrument of salvation. Marriage has been listed as the seventh sacrament for centuries; before the tenth century, it was not. As a sacrament, marriage necessarily comes within the church's exclusive realm of juridical control. It is important to remember that the church considers itself the divinely appointed guardian and interpreter of the divine positive law and the natural law. All sacramental marriages, therefore, should be governed by the precepts of those laws, regardless of the tenets or beliefs of those individuals attempting to contract a sacramental marriage. It is presupposed, for example, that the purposes of marriage are best achieved in a monogamous and indissoluble union.

Canonically, marriage is a contract between a man and a woman who are juridically capable of making this bond. Each partner gives and receives the perpetual and exclusive rights to acts suitable for the generation of offspring. This legalism is applicable to every marriage, because the marriage contract results in a perpetual bond and a relationship sealed by the God who instituted the union.

Christians are reminded that they would be remiss to give a casual dismissal to canon law, no matter how distasteful they found it, and certainly no one would sanction the disobedience of the laws of nature as given by the creator. The Christian sense of marriage is based on divine words that a man and a woman are to be regarded as one, and the belief that when Christ said this he was stating a fact, not merely expressing an opinion. But to be a Christian and also to be married, a woman must have more than mere rules and regulations, or canons of correct behavior. She must understand the true significance that the mystery of Christ, and then the mystery of marriage, hold for her and for the society in which she lives.

Charles Kindregen points out that such an understanding is "sometimes not achieved by 'religious' people because it is a human characteristic that man finds it difficult to maintain his relationship to God without reducing morality to a systematic list of behavioral rules." I have found that the faith of many women has been fundamentalist. Their theology of marriage has been locked into a theology of clerical authority, and so they still tend to hand their marriages over to be treated as the special domain of either the moralist or the canon lawyer.

"Theology at its best imitates the Incarnation," Michael Novak writes. "It does not deal with abstract possibilities, or even abstract imperatives, but with actual history." Marriage, long regarded as a constant, is being evaluated by women today who understand a lot of "actual history." They are often critical. The self-understanding of women, and the ways women have integrated marriage into their lives, have changed radically in the last generation.

The fifties was a time when society assumed, with little or no examination of the merits of such an assumption, that women would automatically relinquish their names upon marriage, that husbands would continue desired careers and support the new family, while their wives would remain at home, anonymous and invisible, doing whatever women did there.

Married women needed no names. Women in our society are given whatever identity they have by virtue of their relationship with men. Una Stannard's work on the history of women's names and their identity as wife gives an illustration. "Memorial tablets asked prayers for the 'soull of Alys late the wyf of Thomas Baldry,' for it was enough to identify her in that manner, just as 'Lot's wife' said who was the wife of Lot, whose own name was never recorded in the biblical chronicles."

For some women the matter of the surrender of their name may seem trivial; after all, there is the very practical concern of the multiple names of future generations. It is, however, a kind of symbol of the basic inequality of marriage right from the beginning.

There are many inequalities. The modern arrangement of marriage has meant for more than a few women the setting aside a hard-earned degree, a profession, along with their dreams and ambitions, for some vague, uncertain time that turned out to be never. Denied any heroine, any other model, women were pledged to the insignificant and the sentimental; they were forced over and over again to invent the wheel.

A new grandmother explained very simply the theology of marriage as it was lived out a generation ago.

> We agreed that night, the night of the proposal, the night of the diamond ring on the appropriate finger, to live together, to establish a home, to put down some roots and raise up some children. We loved each other. We wished God and his Church to bless that love. The Sacrament of Matrimony would give us the grace to carry out the duties of our state in life. This was very sure in some vague kind of way.
>
> In the following weeks we told our parents, visited the parish priest, and obtained a civil license. The banns were read, the champagne was iced, the lilies of the valley were bound in white satin, and one June morning the Monsignor intoned the solemn Introit. "Deus Israel conjugat vos. . . ."
>
> The pastor had seen us briefly, establishing that we had certificates of Baptism and Confirmation, that we were not bound by solemn vows, that the impediments of consanguinity did not exist, and that we intended to enter into an indissoluble union. We assured him solemnly that we would have children if God so willed, and that we would raise as many as God gave us within the Church.

There is no special claim that this was a typical marriage between Catholics of the 1950's, but it was not all that atypical either. Over the past decade hundreds of women who were interviewed agreed, and went on to add that it would never have occurred to them (either then or now) to incite the wrath of God by living together in sin; neither would they have risked the anger of their parents, nor the frowning displeasure of society for a flagrant violation of its norms.

If it is true, as Schillebeeckx claims, that the Fathers of the Council of Trent "violently debated whether the church could intervene in the mutual right of a couple to contract a valid marriage," it is equally true that women of the generation of the fifties took the intervention for granted. They generally believed with Rahner that the sacrament "conveys grace that is God's assistance to us to be loving, true, patient, and brave, unselfish and ready to bear one another's burdens." That was sufficient.

When the pauline letter exhorted them to be submissive to their husbands, they listened passively; raging against the revealed word of God was certainly not permitted. Women consented to be veiled at their wedding, having no historical sense of the meaning of that symbol. Consented is not the right word; custom demanded the veil. As virgins, they were handed over, or "given away" by their fathers (or another male family member) to their husbands. Later, after the births of their children, and it was not infrequent that the birth of a child occurred during the first year of marriage, they would kneel to be "churched," an ancient ceremony reminiscent of the purification of the mother of God. Sixteen years of Catholic education had dictated well.

When the church and the celibate clergy told them that the primary purpose of marriage was procreation, and that true love must be fruitful in children, they were indeed fertile. Holiness of married women and their degree of conformity to the will of God were necessarily tied up with numbers. A woman remembered her fifteenth graduation anniversary: "There was an award for a classmate who had seven children, but the women who had gone on for advanced degrees were simply ignored."

Another woman remembered "requesting permission from my confessor to have an operation that my surgeon felt was imperative. The procedure would have left me sterile." This woman had already given birth to eight children; one could hardly accuse her of selfishness.

When the women of that generation came together, they quietly worried about their husbands having to work at more than one job, not only to buy shoes for 8 or 10 children, pay the dentist and butcher, but also, in some cases primarily, to meet the mounting costs of Catholic education. Of these children for whom so much was sacrificed so that they could sit in parochial school classrooms of 60 or more, one wonders how many attend Sunday Mass today. One woman remarked that

no one ever seemed to believe that it might be arrogant to think that anyone could do good parenting for so many children. No one ever raised the question whether there were those of us who should never be parents at all. And no one ever said out loud that sometimes it hurt that as trained professional women we had given up promising careers to mother these large families. So we talked about pediatricians and PTA groups, the flourishing careers of our husbands, detergent and diapers, and why rhythm did not work. The rituals and beliefs were locked in tightly. And today, our daughters don't even believe us when we tell them how it was.

Another woman found that

it is fascinating to recall how envious brides of the fifties were of their sisters for whom rhythm did work. It was possible to have your children, and to space them acceptably, and still stay within the parameters of Church Law. I never meant to be judgmental of those women, or attribute to them possible materialistic motives, but the fact remains that they were the first ones to have color television, their own cars (not a station wagon) and to take the kids with them for winter vacations in the Caribbean. Most couples with large families never get to do those things. They just survive.

For better or worse, these were the marriages that have yielded the sons and daughters who are marrying today. This was the theology of marriage. The socioeconomic situation of women changed radically in a generation, and so did the church. And we must add the special findings of the social sciences. The insights of the historians and anthropologists have literally bombarded women with information. Questions raised by the radical feminists and the lady-next-door need to be answered, and to be recognized as serious questions. Women now express their right to look to the theologians for new insights, and for insights that are worth having.

The marriage manuals, such as the Reverend George A. Kelly's *The Catholic Marriage Manual* published in 1958, are reminders of the status of women in marriage at that time, and how much has already changed. Father Kelly told his readers that "Nothing gives a man greater satisfaction and sense of fulfillment than a realized sense of importance. Men want recognition. They thrive on it. And their natural instinct in mariage is to be head." (Saint Paul obviously knew what he was talking about!) Kelly goes on to insist that "By virtue of her natural endowments the woman provides the devotion, the self-sacrifice, the tenderness of the family. . . . Her contentment comes from giving herself to husband and children."

Some norms on practical values in marriage are provided, and Father Kelly illustrates the dangers of the working wife. "If the wife's income approximates or exceeds that of her husband, his pride may be deeply wounded, and friction may easily develop over the question of who is the head of the household." Professional status for women may foster undesirable traits, he thinks. Women may become flirtatious, may over-emphasize the importance of dress and adornment, may become economically independent, and "be less willing to make sacrifices and emotional adjustments to keep relations with her husband on a happy basis."

What is tragic is that this rather folksy and probably well-intentioned manual was a reflection of the overall antifeminism found in the more profound and serious clerical authors. There really is no specific commandment in either Testament that reads, "Thou shalt not wound male pride."

A woman social worker who reviewed these quotations, commented bitterly: "There is no ladylike or printable expression that sums up my contempt for Kelly's position. Why are women supposed to reinforce bad behavior?"

A young high school religion teacher dismissed the quotes lightly, saying: "The students in my class would laugh him right out of the classroom." It is no wonder that Reverend James Burtchaell subtitled his work on marriage, "a curious tradition."

Feminist resentment directed at the conservative and chauvinistic position of the Father Kelly's of a generation ago is a fact. This does not mean, however, that women are opposed to sacramental marriage. Kathleen Nyberg thinks:

> It is fairly safe to assume that women are not about to throw over marriage, turn childbearing over to the scientist's test-tube, or child rearing over to the community compound, for the sake of something more. It is not so much a matter of "something more" as it is a need for a new perspective and flexibility for the woman in society.

Equally, it is impossible to assert that the women of today are not women of faith, and that they do not understand that marriage is a sacrament of faith. Their faith is quite vibrant, but of a different quality. It is responsible, not blind, and it is whole. Their faith is not something they possess, but something they are. "Imagine"; Rachel Conrad Wahlberg writes, "the possibilities of such wholeness have not yet entered our fantasies. Who can imagine such sharing? Who can imagine unleashing the possibilities of men and women? Who can imagine such faith?

Women intend to cultivate and live a faith that is not void of reality, but related to reality. Hans Küng writes that women "ought not to believe simply, without verification." The truths of faith always need to be proved and tested by contact with reality, and within the present horizon of women's experience, concretized by reality.

CHAPTER THREE

As Women View Marriage

Helmer: Remember — before all else you are a wife and mother.

Nora: I don't believe that anymore. I believe that before all else I am a human being, just as you are.

Henrik Ibsen

IF MODERN FEMINISM IS ABOUT ANYTHING, IT IS ABOUT HUMAN FREE-dom, a freedom that in its fundamental nature has to do with the whole person. Karl Rahner says that in "real freedom the subject always intends herself, understands and posits herself. Ultimately she does not do something, but does herself." Existing in time and in history, human freedom has a single, unique act: the self-actualization of the person.

Freedom is never merely a given, an allowance. Feminists argue that freedom is not a "dispensation to be gratefully received. It is not a property of one to be given to another. It is not a reward for merit. It is quite simply ours."

Jesus held women and freedom in esteem, but the male theologians who have presided over his church have had some difficulty in following his example. Most feminist writers—Morgan, Daly, Mitchell, Reuther, Heilbrun, Saiving, Fiorenza are merely the beginning of the list—see the Catholic Church as an important and powerful enemy of female liberation, and they have marshalled a mountain of evidence to support their case.

Daly, who holds earned doctorates in both theology and philosophy, lectures that:

> The history of Christian ideology and practice concerning women has been a history of contradictions. In the documents of Scripture, church fathers, popes and theologians throughout the centuries we find an astonishing contrast between, on the one hand, the teachings concerning the value and dignity of the human person and, on the other hand, an all-pervasive misogynism and downgrading of women as persons.

Ruether, calling for the liberation of women within the church, sees the women's movement in general as "engaged in an effort to reach behind the history of civilization to a lost alternative. It seeks to find that root of the alienation which has created the sexist image of the self and society, human beings and nature, God and humanity in patriarchal religion."

Fiorenza, who still identifies with the Catholic tradition, and remains, unlike Mary Daly, within the institutional church, writes that feminist theologians "attempt to bring our feminist analysis and critique to bear upon theology and the Christian church in order to set free the traditions of emancipation, equality and genuine human community which we have experienced in our Christian heritage."

Fascinated by the vision of wholeness, equality and freedom promised long ago in Galatians 3:27ff (There are no more distinctions between . . . male and female, but all of you are one in Christ Jesus.) and given a modern statement in *Gaudium et Spes* of the "exalted dignity proper to the human person," Christian women are impatient and angry when they perceive a lack of consonance in the attitude of the church toward women and in the noble words of its documents. Christian feminists have tended to take the expressions of Vatican II quite seriously.

It must be underlined that feminist theologians do not pretend neutrality because, as Ruether warns, "neutrality hides a commitment to the *status quo*." The *status quo* of Christian theology is definitely white, middle class, and male. Fiorenza writes:

Today's established theologians often feel free to tackle the social, class and race issue, precisely because they belong as males to the "old boys' club," and they themselves are neither poor nor oppressed. They generally do not, however, discuss the challenges of feminist theology, precisely because they refuse to begin "at home" and to analyze their own praxis as men in a sexist profession and culture.

She goes on to argue that only too often the Catholic hierarchy has refused to recognize the authority of women theologians, who may be permitted to function as "tokens" in some seminaries and universities if they do not disturb the male consciousness and structures. Women who demand to be treated as equals are frequently labeled as "aggressive," "crazy," or "unscholarly."

Elizabeth Carroll, R.S.M., writing on women and ministry, says that women today reject role definitions that do not express their total reality or give arbitrary limit to it. Women are "aware of the potential for diverse human development which they share with men. They see their sexuality as a gift but do not accept the role limitations of 'the feminine' imposed upon them by Church and society."

These are a few clips from feminist theologians. They might be summed up in this epigram:

Aristotle, Aquinas, Freud and canon law to the contrary, normal women experience themselves neither as incomplete, mutilated men nor as perpetual children. They experience themselves as intelligent and free, as mature human persons needing, and capable of, creative self-fulfillment on every human level.

Out of the anger that mounts as women understand and are profoundly frustrated by their continual oppression, there has come some freedom of action. Women have begun to exercise some responsible choices, and to reject a childish dependency upon the church. Often they have been quiet and subtle in their reach for freedom, and sometimes there has been a passive or negative quality to their choices. Perhaps they have been sneaky.

There certainly was no sweeping eschatological dimension to it, but sometime during the late sixties, women ceased wearing hats, scarves, veils or some other form (Kleenex?) of head covering when they attended religious services in church. There was no nationally organized crusade by the Catholic Daughters of America urging this rebellion against an ancient custom; there was no rousing protest on a grand scale by the combined Sodalities of the Blessed Virgin Mary; no demonstrations or marches by the Task Force on Women in the Church converged at the door of the Apostolic Delegate or of the Cardinal Archbishop demanding a release from the necessity and obligation of tradition. Women simply stopped.

There may have been a gaggle of calls to the rectory, a flurry of letters to question and answer columnists in the archdiocesan weeklies. Custom and canon were being violated, biblical injunction was blatantly defied, but the clergy at whatever level of the hierarchical structure were hard put to stop the trend. Whatever their private feelings on the subject were, the reverend pastors had to content themselves with what had become an accomplished fact. And the angels, for whose sake women were veiled for centuries, were now left to their own devices.

Almost simultaneously, in the years following the easy availability of effective and relatively safe contraceptive devices, Catholic women quietly began to use several viable means of birth control. The theological writings of the sixties were replete with the pros and cons of the moral issues involved in this kind of family planning. The limitation of conception by artificial means has to be considered as a more sensitive issue, a more intensely personal option, and certainly more culpable than was the question of head covering. The church has taught and still teaches, officially at least, that artificial contraception is an ontic moral evil. It is sin.

Pope Paul VI is said to have anguished over his decision to enunciate his final condemnation of the practice, a wisdom not supported by the commission he had created to study the problem. Women, too, anguished over their decision to risk excommunication, to sin by ignoring the papal teaching that many believed an infallible one, and to assume full moral responsibility for the choice. The anthology *The Experience of Marriage* assembled by Michael Novak in 1964 is a moving testimony to this anguish.

But individual conscience prevailed, and Catholic women now not only use contraceptives, they also approve of them. This autonomous approbation also permits women with a contraceptive mentality to continue to attend Mass and receive the sacraments.

The majority of these women would hardly identify themselves as radicals, or shout with feminist Robin Morgan: "It is an obscenity — an all male hierarchy, celibate or not, that presumes to rule on the lives and bodies of millions of women." Probably most are neither shrewd nor sophisticated enough to see through to the papal anguish. They do not understand that Paul's concern for the life and freedom of individual women and their families was shot through with the dominant need for the preservation of papal authority, whatever the cost.

Other women who have decided, in conjunction with the men they marry, not to have children have learned to dissimulate. Realizing that a priest may not validate such a determined stance or sanction this form of abstention for whatever reason the couple might advance, women lie. No one is saying that this is laudable. What women do say is that the church has no business determining their fecundity, and so has left them little choice. In some instances, it appears that women must cease to be moral in order to be free, or, more accurately, women must cease to believe in such an authoritarian system.

Women whose marriages have died no longer passively accept the inevitability of separation and divorce, followed in either case by the inevitable situation of a life of loneliness and childlessness, or remarriage that perpetually removes them from the life of the church. They are seeking annulments, and getting them, not on the grounds of youthful age, impotence, solemn vows, or the impediments of consanguinity, but because of simulation of consent and lack of due discretion. Tribunal officials know as well as anyone the savage aspects of marriage.

Monsignor Stephen J. Kelleher, a former member of the Marriage Tribunal of the Archdiocese of New York, remembers vividly and with pain the anguish, hostility, fear, and confusion of thousands of couples who came to him when he was presiding judge. "In

almost every instance," he writes compassionately, "the intolerabil-
ity of their marriage had made them destructive of themselves and
each other. They had become destructive of their children." Reverend Jeremiah Kenny of the Baltimore tribunal, pointing to his files,
indicated that they were "simply full of atrocities."

Many women, for whom annulments are not easily available,
and who have exhausted every other means of dealing with the
failed marriage, make use of the internal forum. The question of
the licitness of this procedure is of no concern here but it is being
used, probably by women whose confessors or pastors have understood the irreconcilable differences sometimes caused by adult
character deterioration.

One young woman, the daughter of parents she describes as
devout, plans to marry a divorced man who is seeking an annulment. Their wedding date has already been fixed, and their prefer-
ence and hope is for a Catholic ceremony. "But if the papers do not
come in time," she says, "we will marry anyway, and sacramental-
ize it later if we can." Since American dioceses are granting annulments by the hundreds and in a reasonable length of time, there is
little real concern that this will happen.

Kelleher seems to understand the necessity behind this attitude. He writes:

> A Christian man or woman who has suffered through a
> marriage that actually never was a marriage, or that was a
> marriage but painfully died, has a right to divorce, to marry a
> second time and to remain in full communion with the Chris-
> tian community as well as the civil community. This right to
> marry a second time may even be more demanding than the
> right to marry a first time because of the already awakened
> sense of the need these individuals have for the abiding love
> and affection of a healthy marriage.

Women who agree with Kelleher and who use every avenue
available to enable them to enter into a second marriage (his, hers,
or theirs) and still remain in good faith with their religious heritage
may well be on shaky theological grounds. The degree of dependency, once stolid and stoic, the extent of their conformity to male
standards of what constitutes acceptable behavior and acceptable
faith, have deep and important consequences. Women's security
here and hereafter is a matter of some consequence.

It is out of an almost primal rage that some women finally are able to reverse their dependency and make their own choices, freeing themselves to reflect on their own experiences and human longings. The becoming of women who are truly free implies a transvaluation of at least some values expressed in Christian morality.

Moral theologians may say that women are acting in ways that are contrary to the expressed will of God by bracketing biblical tradition and the secular ideals that have their source in that tradition. Women say that they must create new images and symbols that will bring into being not merely a theology of women, but a more inclusive way of describing all human life.

Freedom is necessarily tough and responsible choosing. Women who choose marriage know with Eugene Kennedy that "basically it is the testing ground on which a person makes it as a human being or not, the risky opportunity for true self-discovery and sharing that makes life more than just bearable." Their expectations of marriage are perhaps greater today than at any other time in history. What Catholic women want, and certainly what they have a right to demand as human persons, is freedom of choice. Women want it from society, but they want it from the church as well. Of course, certain kinds of freedoms are surrendered when any couple marries. What women speak of is the desire to retain the same range of options that their husbands continue to enjoy.

Jesus knew that the intrinsic hope for freedom is not reversible; he lived and proclaimed a new freedom. His teaching was that those who followed him should manifest their freedom by a life of loving service. Family love, conjugal love is a fruitful aspect of that freedom, and women have lived that form of discipleship quite well. Jesus also proclaimed a new freedom from coercive law and meaningless death. We need to include that part of freedom in our Christian thinking.

When the two become one flesh in Christian marriage, it does not mean that the entire identity and freedom of the wife is somehow absorbed in a kind of mystical oneness with her husband. There is iniquity in any intellectual system that insists man and wife are one, and that one is the husband. Man and woman should share a congruous relationship in marriage, one that nurtures freedom and respects it. "We are so both and oneful," as the poet e. e. cummings says.

The church's laws of marriage are independent of individual will, and of any convention or agreement entered into privately by the partners. The couple is pressed into the ancient vintage of an institution that specifies that to which the parties must give consent. Any reservations on the part of the couple are grounds for invalidity of the sacrament. Certainly those in authority in the church should be concerned with the great and often difficult work of the sacrament. It should not be trivialized; the ideals of marriage should not be rendered inconsequential. The celebration of the sacrament should always be serious in its joy; it should be truthful. Disguised obedience has no place here; it never leads to freedom or wholeness.

It is important to remember, however, that obedience to the law has never been considered the highest Christian calling. Love is. Theology must not overstretch or make divine the image and the ideal of the sacrament in such a savage way that all freedom is obliterated.

The desire and will for permanence and the imperative of indissolubility of the marriage covenant are so much a part of the very essence of marriage that the demand has been stated simply: the matrimonial covenant cannot have a sacramental character unless it is accepted initially as definitive and irrevocable. This demand does break down, but not because Catholic couples initially envision marriage as merely a transient liaison. It fails because both men and women approach marriage with different levels of maturity and real commitment to each other, and various degrees of faith in the teaching of the church. Often they need guidance rather than legal decisions. They need acceptance and approval of their existent hopes and fears, and their freedom. And they need to be spared the hypocritical moral calisthenics of having to say yes, when, in fact, they mean no.

Strange as it may seem, it is a fidelity to the faith that is a driving force that requires women, even when it means undercutting church law and tradition, to reevaluate the meaning of the church in their marriages and in their lives, and to demand from the theologians a new synthesis in their teaching that includes women's full freedom as persons.

It is clear from reading the gospels that Jesus respected individual freedom, and that he was deeply concerned with the revelation of the covenant of salvation. It is also clear that he had rather serious reservations about clinging to the letter of the law. If salvation and freedom cannot be extended in all their richness to women, any discussion of sacramental marriage just does not make sense.

If marriage is a sacrament, then it was destined by Christ to be redemptive, and therefore, freeing. Monika Hellwig reminds women that it was designed

> . . . to liberate persons out of the enslavement of fear and meanness into a creative freedom of openness to others and to the future. But the very reasons that demand that marriage be redemptive make it very difficult for it to be so. Marriage partners do not begin out of nothing, they are situated in a history of unfreedom, of unredemption, in a network of human relations that is already badly tangled, with personal experiences in which they have already been betrayed and wounded.

Women who find themselves in a situational history of unfreedom feel that they have been betrayed and wounded. Contemporary theology is not always seen as adequate for modern life. This inadequacy is deplored by women who ask more of the church than their predecessors, women who, through life experiences and education, have been able to transcend the boundaries of a purely female identity, see freedom as the grace that it is.

> Women now stand closer to the juncture of nature and spirit than was possible for most women in the past. They believe in the values of self-differentiation, challenge, and adventure, and are not strangers to that "divine discontent" which has always driven men. Yet these same women value their femininity also; they do not wish to discard their sexual identity but rather to gather it up to a higher unity. They want, in other words, to be both women and full human beings.

The women described by Valerie Saiving may be a small, even elitist group. All women are not exempt from the fear of freedom, any more than were the Israelites who remained in Egypt rather than follow Moses into the Promised Land. Colette Dowling in *The Cinderella Complex* writes, after her interviews and observations, that she has come to the conclusion that "The first thing women have to recognize is the degree to which fear rules their lives."

Women have been programmed to fear independence.

Saiving has a compromise. She suggests that perhaps contemporary feminists are dead wrong, that mothers should rear their daughters with a minimal education in the arts and sciences, and give them little encouragement to be "independent, differentiated, free human beings of whom some contribution is expected other than the production of the next generation." It is a half-hearted, tentative suggestion at best; this is one clock that cannot be turned back. Women have grown into freedom.

If contemporary women do not choose freedom for themselves, the question must still be asked: will they deny it to their daughters?

Chapter Four

Faithfulness in Marriage

*Don't ask me to leave you. Let me go with you.
Wherever you go I will go; wherever you live, I
will live. Your people will be my people, and your
God will be my God. Wherever you die, I will die,
and that is where I will be buried.*

Ruth 1:16-17

ONE OF THE MOST ANCIENT AND INFLEXIBLE THEOLOGICAL TEACHINGS
about marriage is that voluntary sexual intercourse between a married person and someone other than the lawful spouse constitutes
adultery and is a grave moral evil. Constant since Sinai, the divine
imperative, "Thou shalt not commit adultery," has been deeply ingrained in the entire Judeo-Christian tradition.

Biblical teachings on adultery were harsh, at least for women, since their sexual conduct was a crucial factor in a society vitally concerned with family lineage. Leviticus (20:10) describes adultery as a crime punishable by death. Stoning and scourging were common penalties imposed by the Hebrews on an adulterous woman, as in the story of Susanna told in the Book of Daniel.

In the early church, long years of penance were imposed on a wife who cohabited with another man. As an example of the double standard, Pope Pius V, who considered adultery a capital offense, sentenced an adultress to life imprisonment, while a male guilty of the same offense was merely whipped in public. History, as Rosemary Ruether has said with graphic bitterness, "is the holocaust of women."

Theology has rightly insisted that the vows of sacramental marriage create new moral obligations for the covenanting parties. Those who have pledged their troth of faithfulness are under an unconditional obligation to love, honor, and cleave only to each other. Covenants of their very nature demand fidelity.

There is an awesomeness to the solemn vow of fidelity until the couple is parted by death, something quite remote from the sentimental or romantic image of the handsome prince and his fairytale bride living happily ever after. This awesomeness is tied into the reality that faithfulness, for all the esteem it so rightfully deserves, is not always facile. Still, the trusting commitment of fidelity is at the heart of any living marriage. From childhood on, we learned that the keeping of promises was important. Novelist D. H. Lawrence writes that "the instinct of fidelity is perhaps the deepest instinct in the great complex we call sex. Where there is real sex there is the underlying passion for fidelity."

All civilizations, recognizing the honorable person as the one who keeps her word, condemn the traitor and the betrayer, and scorn the person who casually violates a promise for personal gain. But promises are broken, including the sacred promises of marriage. A recent survey in *Ladies Home Journal* reported that one woman out of every five has been unfaithful to her husband. Dominian in *Marital Pathology* cites another study done in the United States that found about one third of all wives had had extramarital affairs.

Fidelity in marriage has frequently, if not universally, been considered as the absence of adultery. It certainly is at least that, and I did not find a single feminist (Christian) who would argue this point. But there are women who would never consider having an affair themselves, nor accommodate their husband's extramarital relationships, but who never seem to care for their spouses in the sense of helping them to grow and actualize themselves. And they do not expect such caring from their husbands. Caring here is used in the sense of "the antithesis of simply using the other person to satisfy one's own needs."

This is not to say that women denigrate the value of physical exclusivity understood as sexual, except perhaps on the ground that adultery is wrong because it is a violation of woman as a man's property. Women know that fidelity means more. The marital bond of faithfulness envisions and ultimately creates a state that transcends the single and binds the history of the couple at the deepest level. It is definitive.

A woman who admitted that she had participated in an extra-marital relationship to ease the quarrels and hostility at home, said: "Adultery isn't wrong because the Church, or even the Bible says so; the whole thing is wrong because it just doesn't work. And God, who is the ultimate pragmatist, knew it all along."

Marriage is a mystery of unity, and devotion to that unique mystery is a valuable, if risky, experience of freedom. Women are concerned about the quality of their marriages and their homes, and they want them to be strong and good. They see fidelity, not as a negation or an absence, but as the active, dynamic reality of love. Eugene Kennedy reflects this attitude when he writes, "People work at fidelity all the time through their consciousness of and responsiveness to each other even when they are apart. Fidelity develops out of a willingness to live in a developing commitment to another human being and there is never anything casual or without significance about it."

The nuptial vows having been exchanged and the union consummated, many couples appear to find that the routines of married life bring problems and difficulties instead of the expected soft summer nights drenched with joy. For some women the major problem of marriage is abuse. The dreams of pleasure turn into nightmares of pain, both physical and psychological. The bride becomes victim.

Some incidents were reported of priest-confessors who told

women penitents, when they complained of their husband's actions, that they should be more loving, more attentive to the needs of their spouse; they should never shun the suffering that conjugal love entails. Love, after all, has always been a difficult and two-edged hazard, as Eugene Kennedy observes, "a vision bedeviled and clouded by self-generated illusions, an ideal never quite fully attained, a motive more compelling for the average man than gold or fame—the prize in the quest for closeness." (Kennedy used these words in an entirely different context.)

Women are reminded of what their mothers and grandmothers have known for generations, that marriage is full of trouble, but that "It is taking the trouble to work at love that makes the difference between successful and unsuccessful marriages." And women said, "Of course."

Confessors and homilists and inhabitants of many rectory parlors spoke to women about grace, the redemptive merits of self-sacrificing love, the blessings to be found in a selfless giving that hides its own pain, and the Christian duties of forgiving wives who will have earned their reward in heaven. Wives were encouraged to meditate upon the thirteenth chapter of First Corinthians, and to strive to emulate the beautiful example of the Holy Family of Nazareth.

One woman, who hid her bruises under long sleeves and behind dark glasses, was lectured on the beneficial results of sincere prayer and reminded that it was a mortal sin to say no.

Another, the wife of a philandering husband and mother of his six children, was told by her confessor, with a reminder of the pauline dictum that the husband is the head of the wife, and that wives should be submissive to their husbands, that she had "made her bed, and now must rest in it." Believing and dutiful, she suffered her panic and her rage. She "worked at love" for three more years, and then, lacking the support of her church in the person of her confessor in terminating her marriage, terminated her life and her child's.

This horror story, unique as it is, cannot be held as normative. It does point out, however, that even religious people can be coldly complacent when they see what happens to some women in marriage, perhaps not wishing to be involved. The church has never advocated the rite of suttee (widow-burning), nor has it subscribed to the Chinese ritual of footbinding. The atrocities of genital mutilation—excision or clitoridectomy, infibulation—were not designed and executed by the African hierarchy, although Mary Daly insists that the "Catholic Church has not taken a clear position against this genital mutilation (which is practiced upon some of its own members)."

If the bruises, the cuts, the broken bones of American wives are not visible in the dark impersonality of the old confessional box, neither are the ruthless ravages of psychological abuse. The wife of a wealthy attorney was hired as a part-time receptionist. There was no economic necessity for this employment, but the children were away at college, and the isolation of an empty house needed relief. Her husband was so incensed at this effrontery that he slammed an expensive vase through a massive picture window. No wife of his would ever work! Submissively, the woman did not return to the position that afforded her a positive sense of independence and worth. Her fidelity must have been at the expense of a great deal of anger and resentment. Prescinding from this personal trauma, the important issue is that the church has done little to expose the husband's action for what it was: infidelity. The viciousness of his stance and of his action was not directed toward the realization of the community of charity in their marriage. And that is savage.

All too frequently, the abuse of women in marriage occurs in the form of physical violence. Lenore Walker in her work, *The Battered Woman*, found the national statistics monstrous. Her research documents that one-third to one-half of all wives are struck, not regularly, but at some time. Accurate determinations of the incidence of wife-beating in America have been difficult to isolate from police reports, court rosters, and hospital emergency rooms because wife-abuse was not an official category on such records. Many such incidents have gone unreported because violence between married partners is considered normal, or at least routine. An assistant States attorney who deals with domestic cases said that the Walker statistics are conservative, and that "It is accurate to state that many American wives are not as safe at home as they are on our crime-infested streets."

Del Martin, author of *Battered Wives*, says that:

> . . . battering is a secret shared by many women who daily fear for their lives. These women bear the brutality of

their husbands in silence because they have no one to turn to and no where to go. They are married women; as such they are untouchable in our society. In the traditional Christian marriage ceremony, the minister warns, "Whom therefore God has joined together let no man put asunder." These words stand between the battered wife and any help she might seek.

Martin cites an instance of a woman who had been whipped, kicked, thrown, and punched. With blackened eyes, a cut face, and a fractured eardrum, she had literally dragged herself to a clergy-man, only to be told that her husband meant no real harm. She was reassured that the battering came from his confusion and insecuri-ty, and that she should "forgive him the beatings as Christ forgave me from the cross."

It remains true that what God has joined, human beings must not arbitrarily put asunder. The difficulty lies in distinguishing when it is God who does the joining at his holy altar, when it is God who sustains a man and woman together in one home, when it is God who blesses one single love. Men and women report a vari-ety of reasons for entering marriage, and as many motivations for sustaining its perpetuation. Social ambition is one, lust, another. Some marry for reasons of economic opportunism, others simply because it is the thing to do. And many marry just to get away from the parental home. They stay married because they just don't know what else to do.

Women need to rediscover the meaning of fidelity and its rela-tion to authentic personal fulfillment, a process that may be full of pain. Janet Golden writes: "Right now there are too many women, just as there are too many priests, who feel that they have promised fidelity without knowing what it meant. Some of them will redis-cover fidelity as freely chosen by themselves, others will not."

Women who are trapped in marriages where there is abuse often find that their desertion, separation, or infidelity to their vows would be economically infeasible, and have little option but to learn a kind of helplessness that is common to concentration camp victims and experimental dogs. With few, if any, marketable skills and several young children to care for, many women are con-cerned that the divided family will live in poverty. Because over one-half of the husbands who are legally required to pay child support and/or alimony do not fulfill that duty, this is not an unrealistic fear. One out of three divorced women in the United States has severe economic problems that stretch beyond their personal needs and include the children they love and for whom they have sole responsibility. The result of this insecurity is that many women remain in the marriage, hoping that somehow it will improve. This is a savage, a tragic dependency.

For those who are more affluent, or who have strong career possibilities, or whose internal resources enable them to choose the option of separation and divorce, there is always the element of human failure to experience and work through. Divorce can be a shattering reality. Madonna Kolbenschlag writes:

> If it frees one from bondage and victimization, it also leaves one with permanent scars and guilt. If there is relief and respite, there is also abandonment and estrangement — loss of some friends, confusion of children, dismay of relatives, loneliness, economic and social jeopardy. Above all, there is the sense of failure and self-doubt that is perhaps the most terrifying and debilitating effect of divorce.

The church, tenaciously defending the words of Jesus on the indissolubility of marriage or the wrong of remarriage, does not approve of divorce. It does not approve of economic want or personal tragedy either, and should not guide its people in those directions. A church that is called "Mother" should not thrust its daughters into an obscene helplessness that is learned, and then becomes learned hopelessness. To the extent that the church retains a brutal and darkly pessimistic stance in the treatment of the failed marriage, it will become little more than an abstraction, with little conformity to the needs of women, and adherence to the true optimism of the Christian teachings on redemption and God's love. Religion should never be as Alfred North Whitehead describes it, "the last refuge of human savagery."

The entrapment of battered women may have several psychological dimensions. For example, some men believe that women are by nature masochistic, but the theological base that snares is still the "hard saying" that Matthew quotes as an uncompromising assertion on the part of Jesus. Over the centuries, at least in the Western Church, this idealized teaching on indissolubility has hardened into inflexible law. All the synoptics record it, and the Council of Trent confirmed the long tradition with its judicial emphasis.

Trent said that the consent to marry, given and received by baptized Christians in the presence of a priest, constitutes a valid and sacramental marriage when the physical union of the couple is consummated. Trent further declared that it is unthinkable that such a marriage could ever be terminated by civil divorce. Separation could be tolerated, but only reluctantly, and no subsequent attempts to remarry were recognized, except as sin.

The exegetical difficulties in dealing with several of the relevant biblical texts, such as the meaning of "porneia" in Matthew 5:32, are problems for the scripture scholars. The texts are equivocal. Few married couples have any sense of the varied history of the sacrament or of the sometimes tortured divisions among the theologians who shape the canons that now control sacramental regulation. If you mention a "theological gloss" to the average Catholic, you draw blank stares.

For those women who suffer the emotional and physical separations that characterize the failed marriage, there is only the law. The belief is that the words of Jesus and the church's canons of marriage intend to defend the principle of the married state. Rosemary Haughton describes what can happen as a result of the rigidity of those laws:

> In the end it became a spider's web in which the human flies struggled hopelessly, becoming faster enmeshed at every effort. The records of cases of ordinary couples who asked for help from canon lawyers when things went wrong are often so appalling that it is easy to obscure the real trouble. The trouble is not the canonists, who are often anguished by their inability to produce a human solution out of the ancient legalisms, but simply the long tradition of non-human mechanistic thinking about human behavior, especially human sexual behavior.

John Meyendorff, writing from the perspective of the Greek Orthodox Church, says that "as a mystery, or sacrament, Christian marriage certainly conflicts with the practical, empirical reality of 'fallen' humanity. It appears, just as the Gospel itself, an unattainable ideal." And one has to wonder if it is not the church's stance on marriage that *really* continues to divide the several Christian communions, rather than the abstruse and technical definitions that stand in the path of true ecumenism.

The recognition that there is a kind of progressive theological paralysis caused by an over-emphasis on legal definition raises the question of whether the church can change its basic canon law of marriage so that "the evangelical injunction concerning the permanence of marriage can be observed as an ideal rather than a legal absolute." Leonardo Boff asks, "Can the sacramental reality be held to be always one and the same thing, or can it exist on different levels of perfection and in different degrees of wholeness?"

But while Peter Huizing interprets the legal discussion of marriage and divorce in Matthew 19:1-9 and comments that Jesus "did not speak about a law imposed from without, but about human life itself and its inner meaning," and the Canon Law Society struggles to be obedient to the tradition and still satisfy the pastoral needs of the suffering, the human tragedies multiply.

Michael Novak, in his observation on the status of contemporary marriage, asks: "How many couples do not truly love one another? . . . How many marriages have a merely legal union? And are such marriages, whatever canon law might say, profoundly inhuman and immoral?" The beauty of marital fidelity, disturbed or shattered either by human limitation or serious sin, is altered. What should happen then cannot be deduced simply and solely from what the bible has to say about marriage.

Marriage canons were based on a post-tridentine theology concerned principally with organization, institutionalization, and codification. But marriage is not only about men and law, it is also about women and love.

Sheila Collins writes about theology and women in Appalachia. She remembers attending a seminary and studying the works of men "who never have to change and wash dirty diapers, sit for six hours in the welfare office, stay up all night with a sick child, pick cotton in a dusty field, sell their bodies for a living, or work all day in the mills and then come home to do the dinner, the laundry and the dishes." Her thesis is that if a theology of marriage is to be meaningful for women today, it must not begin with the abstractions of male scholars, but with the stories of women.

Many women in the church are now sincerely convinced that the old wineskins of canon law are too brittle and sour to contain the fresh wine of marriage as women envision it in the modern world. Experience suggests that Catholic women who cannot discover effective and morally acceptable solutions to problems that seriously affect their marital happiness may adopt secular solutions.

Changes in the church, one woman remarked, have always come about after the people have changed already. "The young people are saying 'no' to the legalisms that do not make a marriage or guarantee fidelity of any kind. Now they are simply living together, or they obtain a civil license. Maybe later they will consider having their union blessed in the Church."

Maybe they won't.

Chapter Five

Fertility and Marriage

Be fruitful, multiply, fill the earth. . . .

Genesis 1:28

The primary purpose of marriage is the procreation and education of children.

Code of Canon Law, 1013-1

"LOVE MUST BE FRUITFUL IN CHILDREN," KARL RAHNER WRITES IN HIS homily on marriage. "Marriage accepts this possibility, uncalculated and unplanned: it accepts it from the living God."

51

The absoluteness of this canonically and biblically based teaching has been given its modern classical form by Pope Paul VI in his encyclical, "On Human Life."

Marriage is not, then, the effect of chance or the product of evolution of unconscious natural forces; it is the wise institution of the Creator to realize in mankind his design of Love. By means of the reciprocal personal gift of self, proper and exclusively to them, husband and wife tend towards the communion of their beings in view of mutual personal perfection, to collaborate with God in the generation and education of new lives.

Pope Paul VI wrote his controversial letter in 1968 against the advice of his own specially appointed commission, and it fractured the church. That is history. Pope John Paul II has continued to insist upon the correctness of his predecessor's position, an opinion that the magisterium has maintained for some time.

While much of the divisiveness, and not all of it among lay people, has centered around the moral judgment of the papacy that artificial means of birth control are not sanctioned by the church, we must also contend with the stark and fundamental imperative contained in the canon and affirmed by papal authority: every married woman must bear children. This is a sacred and ancient axiom, too holy and too old to question.

On one level, this imperative is not to be regarded as excessively harsh and punitive. Marriage and eventually motherhood seem to be the answer to every young girl's prayer. In any case, it is a fact that in 1974 the United States Census Bureau reported that 95 percent of all women age 35 and older had been married at least once, and all but ten percent of these women had mothered at least one child. These figures seem to sustain the argument that most American women have wanted to marry, did marry, wanted to have children, and had them.

It is also evident that women have gone to sometimes incredible lengths to become fertile; witness the significant number of women who undergo testing, surgery, artificial insemination, drug and psychotherapy, and who now stand in line, full of hope in the technique that can implant a test-tube baby. Sterile women, frequently an object of contempt or pity, haunt the adoption and foster parent agencies looking for a child.

Single women who adopt children, sometimes preferring motherhood to wifehood, constitute a new group of mothers. Women who bear children out of wedlock are now keeping their progeny, conceived in passion, or by incest, or rape. And when all else fails, it is now possible to hire a surrogate mother to carry to term the husband's seed.

Mothering has been viewed as intrinsic to the nature of women, as evidence and proof and validation of competence as a female. Motherhood is a powerful urge, a fundamental and often mysterious desire, even an imperious demand more central to the preservation of humankind than any other special calling. The very name of the sacrament that renders motherhood licit is derived from the Latin root "mater," mother.

Theologians say that Christian marriage exists to afford people a share in creation and redemption. Historically, they justified marriage and sexuality with some misgivings; religion and "carnality" were conflicting forces. There was the obvious necessity that the race be propogated, and the divine command given in Genesis 1:28 to "be fruitful, and multiply, and fill the earth . . ." needed to be obeyed. Theology also recognized that the special calling of women and men to a state of lifelong virginity was not given to all.

The structures and arrangements of marriage have responded to vastly divergent human needs and societal conditions over the centuries. But it is incontrovertible that all human life is of woman born; there is, at least at this period of history, no other choice.

The biological constant has become an institutional constant, and one that aims at ensuring that women shall remain under male control and domination. Adrienne Rich in *Of Woman Born* shows how the institution of mothering has been crucial to diverse and political systems. She contends that "It has withheld over one-half the human species from the decisions affecting their lives; it exonerates men from fatherhood in any authentic sense; it creates the dangerous schisms between 'private' and 'public' life; it calcifies human choices and potentialities."

The bitterly repressed unconscious needs of women have erupted before in history, particularly the need to choose, but the eruption was fragmented. Now it surfaces with greater clarity. Women view marriage and maternity from a new perspective, and this gives rise to some profound questions about the nature of marriage and its purposes, and about the needs of the partners in each unique union.

One question is about the validity of holding that the need or compulsion to maternity is, in fact, axiomatic and universal. If Pope Pius XII was correct when he said, "Now a woman's function, a woman's way, a woman's natural bent is motherhood," then all women are indeed called to bear and nurture children, in marriage, of course. The logic is flawless. Some feminists, however, believe that the tacit initial premise is in error. Inbred desires and socialized needs, they think, are not less powerful than natural and instinctual ones. Processing women to want children has been the goal of practically everyone and everything — parents, grandparents, schools, churches, the law, the media, and even governmental policy.

Angela McBride has a blistering statement.

> I remember with bitterness that "our mother" the church told women for two thousand years (more or less) that their mission in life was to have children. That was the only purpose of marriage and their existence . . . No love. Absolutely no sex without an eye to procreation. The mother of God coredemptress with her son. The mother of the children of men to be Mary's handmaiden on earth — to sacrifice herself to lead the little ones to Christ. That makes me sick . . . I think I've been so "mad" I avoided having children as a resistence measure. How dare they reduce me to a servant status. Mary's handmaid indeed! Who is she that she should be a model for me?

There is an immense amount of anger in the words of this woman, a rage directed at the teaching of the church regarding the purpose of marriage and the mission of women. Christian women may disagree with her theology, holding that self-sacrifice is an integral part of any Christian commitment. Jesus himself came among us as a servant. But Christian feminists will not argue with her bitterness and its attendant destructiveness. A human, not an animal, act is at stake.

Feminists believe that the vision of Mary and her "handmaidens" is an antiquated and romantic notion that is best ignored. But more importantly, they hold firmly that the coercion to bear children is radically inhuman, impersonal, and a violation of Christian love.

The rebelliousness of women is probably not so much against motherhood itself, but against the ways motherhood has been institutionalized. No other relationship calls forth such a multiplicity of expectations, emotions, and demands as the mother-child one. In the beginning, it is the whole world for us. Nancy Friday observes, "In our beginnings is our essence." It is an impressive role, and one difficult to perform.

In her work, *The Future of Motherhood*, sociologist Jessie Bernard notes:

> Women are daring to say that although they love children, they hate motherhood. That they object to being assigned sole responsiblity for child care. That they object to having child care conceived as their only major activity. That they object to the isolation in which they must perform the role of mother, cut off from help, from one another, from the outside world.

Bernard is not alone. M. Esther Harding theorizes that the role of mother seems doomed in advance. Mothers are blamed for everything from juvenile delinquency to adult neuroses to unrealized potential to vandalism to communism and other assorted woes of contemporary society. The blame hangs forever on the shoulders of the maternal figure. That is the "bad" mother. On the other hand, "good mothers" are also accused, by their devotion and skillful handling of their sons and daughters, of binding their offspring to themselves in an "inescapable fixation, a stifling symbiosis."

Angela Barron McBride reaffirms Harding's contention, calling motherhood, "Mission Impossible: shaping a child who is healthy, adventuresome, happy, sensitive, intelligent, attractive, creative, sociable, kind, generous, ecology-minded, brave, polite, spontaneous and good—all at the same time." It is no wonder that McBride concludes that mothers, who are not saints, often speak of frustration.

Motherhood means pregnancy first, means giving birth, and for some women means lactation. It means disturbed sleep for many weeks and months, anxiety over illness (really, a slight fever will do it), tending to childish wishes and correcting adolescent wildness, and then, finally, it means standing by and learning not to interfere. But over and beyond all this, as Harding reminds women:

For the woman who is aware of the psychical realm, maternity imposes a discipline which reaches below the surface and strikes directly at her most hidden, most secret selfishness and egotism. The child's physical welfare depends upon her, but she has a deeper and more fundamental responsibility than that for his body. She must bestir herself and put her own psychological house in order if she is not to jeopardize his soul.

Dorothy Dinnerstein in *The Mermaid and the Minotaur* discusses the divisions of responsibility, opportunity, and privilege between men and women, and finds a core fact: "the fact of primary female responsibility for the care of infants and young children." She attacks the current gender arrangements not only as punitive to women, but also as disastrous for the children as well. She shows how female dominated child care perpetuates a double standard of sexual behavior, and how this guarantees certain antagonisms against women. Men, including churchmen, assume that women exist as a

> natural resource, an asset to be owned and harnessed, harvested and mined, with no fellow-feeling for her depletion and no responsibility for her conservation and replenishment. Finally, they include a sense of primitive outrage at meeting her in any position of worldly authority.

Dinnerstein goes on to demonstrate how the concept of primary-care-motherhood will reliably give us childish men, because as boys they were unsure of their grasp on life's primitive realities. "And it gives us girls who will reliably grow into childish women, unsure of their right to full worldly adult status."

Jessie Bernard agrees with this prediction. She sees the children of the women "struggling to fill their lives with the mother role" as much victimized as the mothers were.

The way that mothering has been institutionalized is not an unchanging transcultural universal; this role is an historical product. Feminist scholars such as Nancy Chodorow believe that the primary care of young children by women has been merely functional, and functional for a system founded on sexual inequality, and not for social survival, let alone free human activity. She claims:

Children could be dependent from the outset on people of both genders and establish an individuated sense of self in relation to both. In this way, masculinity would not be tied to denial of dependence and devaluation of women. Feminine personality would be less preoccupied with individuation, and children would not develop fears of maternal omnipotence and expectations of women's unique self-sacrificing qualities.

The pattern of life for mothering women that places them in this fixed role has been not only useful but necessary for the well-being of a society that is based on the professional division of labor and production for profit. It is political, as Kate Millet says. The pseudo-glorification or mystification of women, first as love-goddess and then as madonna, keeps a woman in a place or role by making it her fate, the old "anatomy is destiny" thing.

Women are regarded as child-breeders by nature, vocationally far removed from the sordidness of the public sphere, and therefore restrained from ever becoming a public force. Number one "Moms" are usually not regarded as creatures of rational discourse. It's a pretty gloss, but the mystification actually treats women as closer to animal than human nature.

Hilde Hein, writing in the same vein, opposes the reduction of women to a mere instrument of procreation. She decries the "cult of motherhood as an oppressive and deceptive exploitation of women, alienating inasmuch as it contracts the whole person into a single, utilitarian and very limited function."

Can this really be the mind of the Lord?

Intrinsic to the issue of the imperative to procreate is the children themselves. In our society, offspring are no longer a strong economic advantage as they had been when the culture was more agrarian. Past generations of parents had learned that the more children they produced, the greater the likelihood that many would live to maturity, and more help would be available for the innumerable chores. Also, it was apparent that in a time devoid of the financial benefits of social security and medicare, aging parents had to be dependent upon large numbers of children for their support during their declining years. These were hardly generous, self-sacrificing reasons for large families.

Today, however, children may be an expensive liability, a luxury only the rich can afford. The direct cost of rearing and educating a middle-class child in America in 1977 was a staggering $64,000. This sum is more formidable if the foregone income of the mother is calculated into the total.

Bernard Haring laments that today "children are neither useful nor necessary in the ordinary family." He is sensitive to the social and economic pressures that have brought about this shift in values, and calls for responsible parenthood motivated by generosity and the witness of mutual love.

Haring grants that there has been a forward progress in the theology of marriage from the time of *Casti Connubii,* written in 1930 by Pope Pius XI, to the marriage documents of the Second Vatican Council in 1965, but realizes that there are still unresolved questions.

For example, some couples define responsible parenthood to mean not having children. None. None ever. Reasons cited for this anti-children stance are sometimes economic or medical, but some couples believe that this planet cannot endlessly provide food and water capable of sustaining a population that doubles every few generations, that our air and oceans are already badly polluted, and other natural resources are significantly depleted. Some couples are conscious of the lack of adequate housing, the collapse of the job market, of increased crime and delinquency that has moved to include the more affluent suburbs as well as the cities, and the constant threat of nuclear disaster, all of which combine to make a world unfit for new life.

David Thomas, Director of the National Institute for the Family, also raises the issue of an anti-children climate in American society, and finds it disturbing. Couples seem to want to live their lives without the disturbance and interference of children. He thinks that "greater affluence, more ease of travel, more attractions outside the home all contribute to a person wanting these instead of something or someone else."

Dr. Seana Hirschfeld, a practicing psychotherapist, comments that if a couple finds that children are an unnecessary and undesirable part of their life together, they should not attempt to become parents for the simple reason that they will be bad parents. Women practicing psychotherapy and social work are frequently more selective than God and/or the church in their advice to the newly married.

The ecological concern about overpopulation and its attendant problems is cited by Father James Burtchaell as the rationale some couples offer for their childlessness. This formula and this reserve, he thinks, are the formula and reserve of the wealthy "who plead with or pay or sterilize poor people (and nations) not to have so many children because they, the wealthy, know there are things ever so much more important than children." He suggests that the wealthy are resistant to the expenditures of the welfare organizations. In a rush of alliteration, he continues:

> Couples are chary of children because they are a burden. A child claims one's heart and drains one's substance, and then grows up and goes away, without your being sure the child will bring you pride or chagrin. Most obviously, a child costs cash and comfort and convenience.

Sally and Phillip Scharper see ecological concern that results in the decision for childishness from a different perspective. In their article, "The Future of the Family," they recognize that the doubling of the world population by the year 2000 will ravage an already plundered planet. They believe that this knowledge will cause most young parents to choose to bear a very limited number of children.

> Some indeed, may make the extremely heroic decision to have no children at all, becoming "eunuchs for the sake of the Kingdom," understood as the building of the earth into a fit dwelling place for that sacred creature made in the image of God.

Theologians, it is hoped, will come to recognize the theological dimension to ecology, remembering that humanity is steward over all creation, and that the church is a guardian of the quality of life. God gave us a degree of intelligence, and it must be presumed that he expects us to use it. The Scharpers write:

> In the context of the ecological crisis the Church might well exhort the married to limit the number of their children to one or two, a sacrifice to be made in the interest of "the greater good," a concept that has long been a hinge concept in scholastic philosophy and Catholic moral theology. For those

capable of "a yet more excellent way," the Church may recommend having no children, for theological reasons not too dissimilar from those long advanced to support priestly celibacy and the religious vow of chastity.

Students and analysts of our society believe that childless marriages are likely to increase in incidence. Dr. Albert J. Dudley, Jr., reflecting on his practice in gynecology, said, "I see quite a few couples who choose to remain childless, and who make that choice permanent."

Strong and autonomous women, who are able to resist the coercive pressures to become mothers, insist that the decision to remain childless is a sound moral decision. Statistically, childless marriages are more prone to divorce. Lack of offspring eases the emotional trauma of separation, and the financial burden on the husband is less onerous. But the childless marriages that do survive, contrary to all the cliches, are reported as happier than marriages with children. Jessie Bernard advances the data:

> Mothers far more than childless wives find marriage restrictive. Far more, expectably of course, report problems in the marriage; considerably fewer report satisfaction in the marital relationship; and more feel dissatisfied with themselves.

At a recent meeting of the regional Association of Women Deans and Counselors, 18 women from colleges and universities situated in the Middle Atlantic states met to discuss particular problems they encountered with women students. From their academic vantage point, these deans had listened to bright women undergraduates proclaim adamantly that when, and if, they married, they did not intend to have any children. One woman counselor, who knew perfectly well that years and a loving husband may change the student's mind, still worried, "Does this mean that only the dummies will become mothers?"

An additional piece of evidence that points out the existence of this trend came in 1980 from Dr. Carol Ehrlich, Assistant Professor of American Studies at the University of Maryland at Baltimore County. She has accumulated data that indicate that 10 percent of women between the ages of 13 and 35 intend to remain childless.

Certainly the materialism and selfishness that have concerned recent pontiffs and disturbed theologians such as Thomas and Burtchaell are not Christian virtues. Probing the motivation of any individual woman to remain infertile may indeed reveal a bankruptcy of generosity, a poverty of love, and a lifeless faith. But not always.

Current information from the social scientists is available to indicate that one of the major causes of marital breakdown is mental illness and severe personality disorder. Alvin Toffler, commenting on the litany of current social problems being addressed by social workers and the mental health industries, says:

> In Washington a President's Commission on Mental Health announces that fully one-fourth of all citizens in the United States suffer from some form of severe emotional stress. And a National Institute of Mental Health psychologist, charging that almost no family is free of some form of mental disorder, declares that psychological turbulence . . . is rampant in an American society that is confused, divided and concerned about its future.

Toffler is not reporting on the severe varieties of illness that totally destroy a person's capacity to reason and place acts of choice, but rather on the neuroses that impoverish life and imprison the personality. These are the "hollow men," immortalized by T. S. Eliot and explained by Rollo May. The people May sees in his office complain of emptiness, of vacuity, and of a lack of power to change their lives. "Many people," he says, "do not know what they want; they often do not have any clear idea of what they feel."

Barbara Fiand makes a similar observation. "The person who shifts and fluctuates or even the one who holds her position out of compulsion of insecurity . . . cannot understand because she is afraid to love. The one who is incapable of loving herself cannot risk loving the other."

The question is: Should such a person risk creating a child?

Christopher Lasch has written some 400 pages, followed by an impressive bibliography, to sustain his contention that Americans live in *The Culture of Narcissism*. Snell and Gail Putney in their work, *The Adjusted American*, show how our families are influenced by neurotic patterns. Founded on notions of romantic love and the search for indirect self-acceptance, American marriage, they contend, seeks the impossible dream.

The adjusted American seeks in marriage that which it cannot offer — a working substitute for self-acceptance — and often fails to find the mutual need for satisfaction that marriage can facilitate. Stripped of many of its early economic and social functions by industrialization and urbanization, and called upon to fulfill an impossible emotional function, the American family founders in conflict.

Today's bookstores present a plethora of paperbacks in their psychology sections that attempt to address in a popular way the needs and problems of our time. And they sell, presumably to the individuals described by Toffler, May, and the rest.

Pastor-counselors seek advanced degrees and postgraduate courses and workshops in techniques and therapies that they hope will make their work more effective.

The extensive writing of Andrew Greeley in sociology and Eugene Kennedy in psychology is remarkable because these men have attempted to integrate their own disciplines with theology. Many theologians, however, show little background or sensitivity to the studies in these areas.

Jack Dominian thinks that after baptism and the eucharist, marriage is the most important sacrament in the church because it is the daily means of salvation for so many. He also published a series of articles in the *British Medical Journal* that have been combined in the slim volume, *Marital Pathology*. By the time he is finished with such problems as anxiety, depression, insomnia, obsession, alcoholism, histrionicism, and drugs, one wonders whether any marriage, intensely scrutinized, could not be found null and void.

In an earlier work, Dominian says that "with the passage of time, the wife of a neurotic husband tends to become more like him on the basis of the interaction in which her life becomes increasingly constricted, isolated from friends and social activities, and concentrated on the needs of her husband." Common sense would seem to dictate that the fragility of the persons involved in such a marriage, and there are countless such couples, may mean that the conjugal union was a risk from its inception. To increase the risk by the inclusion of children in the family is simply to court disaster. A credible theology must evidence a real concern for the values essential to human life and growth.

A psychiatric social worker reported the case of a young and seemingly healthy bride who developed a severe prepartum psychosis just a few months after her marriage. The attending physician inquired why the couple had opted for parenthood so soon after their wedding. Both husband and wife reminded him of the teaching of the church regarding birth control as well as the primary purpose of marriage. Although marriage preparation programs, at least according to one Family Life Director, do not advocate such immediacy, this couple accepted the official, papal teaching that the conception and birth of a child should be regarded as an act of faith.

Feminist writers with no sense of reverence for such authority might say that women need to move beyond magic and superstition and blindness toward the reaches of adult and independent faith.

Burtchaell says: "People who think that this bunch of Christians is generally sensible and sober about its religion, but a little peculiar in its views on matrimony are really quite wrong. We are crazy in every way."

What is difficult is that the church does and will recognize as sacramental at least some marriages, knowing that the union will never come to fruition in children because of some physiological disorder. So physiological incapacity is acceptable, psychological incapacity is not. Priests must be assured that the couple does in fact intend to have children (this before the ceremony is permitted); any other intent would render the marriage invalid.

A problem that modern women who are intent upon a career encounter when they consider the prospect of maternity is that of age. Strong commitments to a career are difficult for women to make until they know the person they are going to marry. Many professional women delay marriage until they have completed their professional preparation, and so they marry later in life. Generally, they marry a man of comparable age or older. The contemporary couple is quite aware of the factor that age plays, the age of either or both parents, in influencing the probabilities of giving birth to a child with genetic defects.

Relieved of the ancient fear of dying in childbirth (it was no accident that the skull and crossbones were carved into the headboard of the marriage bed several centuries ago), women are now faced with the prenatal anxiety, and sometimes the known reality, that their unborn child will be damaged. They also realize that the damaged body will live on, because of medical advances and life-saving techniques, years longer than might have been expected even a generation ago. Reluctance to conceive or to continue a pregnancy under these conditions might not be considered a sublime act of faith in God's loving providence, but it may well be an honest assessment of woman's potential and capabilities.

One woman who wanted to marry but never did, said that her reason stemmed from a real terror of repeating the experience of her own mother who had given birth to an epileptic child, and another who was severely retarded. This woman would have been happy to adopt, and the man she hoped to marry was understanding and agreeable. But no priest was willing to witness such a marriage as sacramental, and they were chided for lack of faith and courage. Ironically, it was a strong kind of faith and courage that sustained them through the loneliness and deprivation of their adult years. Such a waste of love is savage.

Another young bride spoke of growing up in a home plagued by chronic illnesses that were hereditary. "I think my parents are saints," she said. "But I've lived with cancelled vacations, monstrous medical bills, and, more importantly, parents who were drained both physically and emotionally. I'm not going to be a martyr day in and day out. I just don't have my mother's strength, or maybe I don't want to find out that I do."

Loving women do not believe that any child should come into the world as a consequence of lust or unplanned sexual pleasure. Birth is a profound event, and one should neither be an accident nor a duty. Feminists believe that childbirth must be seen as the rich fruit of the commitment of two people who call, with God, an already loved child into being.

And for those women, clearly the majority, who will want and will bear children, there is the prevailing mentality of contraception. It is no new thought that the emergence of "the pill" as a relatively safe and accurate birth control agent has changed the lives of modern women more than any other single event. Today's brides might be more inclined to canonize Allen Guttmacher and John Rock and Robert Kristner than Pope Paul VI and the Roman Curia.

The pill is seen as a metaphor for the newly discovered autonomy of contemporary women. Madonna Kolbenschlag describes a new woman, and one who is no longer anathema in the general tenor of the times.

In assuming more independent control over her body, the "new woman" declared her right to control her own time, life-span, life-style and self-image. She was no longer hostage to the implacable forces of fertility, social mythology and dogmatism. She need no longer be sacrificed to the unknown gods of nature, no longer driven to self-mutilations in defending the integrity of her life. She began to experience a wider spectrum of options, the kind men have always taken for granted. She began to choose, and thus to grow.

American Catholic women of childbearing years use contraceptives right along with their Protestant, Jewish, and nonreligious sisters. The attitude is that prolonged voluntary sexual abstinence as an option may result in the unity of the emotional bond being endangered. They fear that to attempt such abstinence will create an atmosphere of tension, irritability, and a withering coldness. And too many brides have heard the moans of their mothers that "rhythm just doesn't work."

Joan Bel Geddes points out that families have always attempted to control their size, "and the means they used were much less fastidious than swallowing a pill: witches' potions, abortions, child abandonment, exposure, and infanticide."

Andrew Greeley, in touch with the pulse of the American Church, says:

In the early and middle '60's, while Pope Paul hesitated, a substantial proportion of Catholic married people turned to the Pill. Then, in 1968, the pope belatedly ruled against their choice. Few clergy or laity listened. Then they discovered, as Catholics in many other countries did long ago, that no one was going to drive them out of the Church because they dissented. After that it became easy. I'm not saying that such behavior is proper or moral or Catholic. I'm saying that it is happening, and that it has become typical.

Pope John Paul II, glowing and healthy in the brilliant sunshine of Washington at the end of his American tour in the autumn of 1979, spoke of the evils of contraception and even the contraceptive mentality. The same day on the evening news, Americans saw a young mother with a child in each arm and a belly full of another.

The woman appeared frail, a gaunt refugee; she was one of the boat people. An American woman cried angrily, "I would like to see the Pope look that woman in the eye and tell her that contraception is wrong." She thought that would be savage.

Catholic women, regardless of the official teaching on *Humanae Vitae* and the counsels of the present pontiff, are women with a contraceptive mentality. There is little ambivalence on this point. Perhaps in another period of history, perhaps after yet another global conflict when families will sacrifice beloved sons and daughters for national pride or greed at worst — national honor at best — then fertility might have to be encouraged, but not now. Pontifical pronouncements notwithstanding, American women are not returning to a life of endless pregnancies and lactations; they will not, in general, endure the emotional and financial strains that inexorably grow and proliferate for large families in our times.

On a nationally televised Phil Donohue Show, a woman, with raw and naked honesty, told the audience: "The only reason I'm a mother is because I'm a Catholic." Her sincerity was respected, but her reason was wildly repudiated.

The church left the brides of the fifties with little choice but to bear children or to sin. Most women in history have become mothers without any real choice, and quite a few have lost their lives in the process. The knowledge seems long in coming, but women today proclaim that true motherhood does not admit to coercion.

Chapter Six

Identity in Marriage

But the Lord answered: "Martha, Martha," he said, "you worry and fret about so many things, and yet few are needed, indeed only one.

Luke 10:41

THE IMMENSE IMPORTANCE OF THE FUNCTION OF PARADIGMATIC INDI-viduals in the development of the person has been underlined by many contemporary writers. Identity formation has a great deal to do with a woman's past identification with significant others, and with the fusion of these identifications into a new integration. Identity formation also involves identifications with groups as well as individuals: the family unit with all its traditions and specific mores; the ethnic roots and religious affiliation; social class, nationality, and time of birth — and, of course, gender.

Michael Novak contends that "individuals seldom, if ever, act according to principles and rules stated in words and logically arranged. They act, rather, according to models, metaphors, stories and myths. Their action is imitative rather than rule abiding."

For Max Scheler, the model, the Vorbild, is an important stimulus for the development of the person. In giving his ontic definition of the exemplar, Scheler emphasizes this aspect of being as a "demand of ought-to-be." He says, "It is more by following an exemplar than by following norms that a person is formed and molded in his moral behavior and being."

Agreement comes from Kai Nielsen, who suggests that "for the most part, people get their standards not from ethical treatises or even scriptural texts or homely sayings, but by idealizing and following the examples of some living person or persons."

Models for American women abound.

Television and the current slick fashion magazines reach millions of women daily with their "ought-to-be" message. Women on television are generally glamorous creatures featured on the soap operas who move from luxurious condominiums through torrid affairs to an "open marriage" with a handsome husband who is also a millionaire, or at least a doctor.

On the commercials, women appear guilt-ridden because he has "ring around the collar." They accuse themselves of having failed miserably as wives with good communication skills when they discover they did not know just how much their husbands "cared" about the whiteness of his laundry, or that they were unaware he preferred stuffing to potatoes. Ecstatic about a new hair coloring—expensive, but "I'm worth it"—in great glee over the news of a breakthrough in feminine protection forms, the ladies are not "thrilled" with either their laxatives or drain cleaners.

Carol Bradford of "Eight Is Enough" has a lifestyle few middle-class American women could even hope to compete with; one wonders how many women, and especially Black women, can possibly identify with Louise Jefferson. Sunday night super-mother Ann Romano of "One Day at a Time" is decorative and divorced. "Alice" is a widow, who, noting the brevity of the human condition, had to "get out from under."

Television's sisters of the slick magazines are consumers par excellence. They are enlightened consumers, of course, because the magazines want to stylize the women they reach as thoughtful and sophisticated. Madison Avenue profoundly believes that women must be liberated, but the fine print of this creed reads: freedom is contingent upon the desire for new products. The young, suburban housewife is no frump; she is invariably shown as vitally concerned about her home and children, and possessed of abundant time and intelligence for the consideration of such critical issues as the merit of a coating mix for pork chops and the ultimate quality of toilet paper.

Catholic women do not necessarily close the glossy cover or shut off the machine that urges them to stay slim, use a mouthwash and deodorant, become a blonde, smoke a woman's cigarette. Like everyone else, they receive the message that if they do all these things, purchasing an endless number of products in the process, they will be able to snare a man, marry him, and then live happily ever after. "Whoever makes the labels, holds the power," Philip Slater says, with a reminder that all these devices have been invented by men who seem to prefer women who are young, thin, made-up, and under 30, the age of disaster.

Another model for American women, and a relatively recent one, is that of the career-oriented woman. Women have been active in the business world and in the professions to some extent and for some time; the current economic situation, if nothing else, has proliferated their numbers. The average bride in the fifties, as has been shown, expected to relinquish her career upon marriage, or at least upon maternity, and to become the "happy housewife heroine" so graphically described by Maxine Schnall in *Limits*. A generation later, almost half of the married women in America gave up decorating their dream houses and chauffeuring their children to the orthodontist and returned to the work force, including almost half of the women who have children under 18 years of age.

Ignace Lepp, a French priest and psychotherapist, had no doubt that love plays a primordial role in women's lives, and said that even for the well-educated, the great success of their lives and realization of their destiny would be expected from love. He reflects that many men have been successful in combining a love affair with their social and professional lives, but that few women have been able to do so. "Most women," he writes, "who have been successful socially and professionally, are either spinsters or unhappily married."

American brides of today do not often believe this. They want marriage and a career, hazard or not. With multiple degrees and impressive titles, women are moving slowly into the domain of male power and creativity.

It is a seductive model, and one that can be wildly demanding. In a 1980 study of highly successful women, Paula Span states the fact that "not only do these women put in at least fifty to sixty hour weeks, but they are likely to devote a chunk of their leisure time to earning the credentials that will propel them upward." Span describes a typical Sunday in the life of a woman who is in management and taking accounting courses at night. Sunday is the day she takes time out to prepare a gracious dinner for her husband. "At the end of the meal . . . I always tell him, 'Nice seeing you. See you next Sunday.' " Needless to say, this situation can be deadly for a family life that requires support and nurturance and companionship for its survival.

The career-marriage woman may have to endure long separations from her family, traveling alone, dealing with men who are still faintly amused at or openly antagonistic to the thought of a woman executive. Arrangements to accommodate the working wife and mother may mean frozen dinners and fast foods. Long distance decisions about children might have to be made. Career women frequently have to fight traffic, discrimination, slurs, propositions, and ulcers. But some women, wearing the suit, pumps, and gray-rimmed glasses, and carrying the appropriate leather briefcase, find it all means fulfillment.

There is the traditional model of the wife-mother, immaculately groomed at 7:00 A.M. and icing the compote in which she will serve freshly squeezed orange juice. She will send her children off to school with nourishing breakfasts and protective outerwear, and then joyfully anticipate their return home (with straight A's in math and a letter in track) by baking several batches of chocolate chip cookies.

This model woman jogs, does needlepoint, is a gourmet cook, and mixes a perfect dry martini. She belongs to the PTA, drives her own station wagon, reads the books on the current best-seller list, and dances cheek-to-cheek with her husband at the Knights of Columbus dance. Rollo May describes her as the good wife who is "good by not doing things—by not complaining when her husband works late, by not fussing when a transfer is coming up, by not engaging in any controversial activity." She is the modern Ruth.

Many women cast in this role have found its rewards paltry. Theirs is a world of harshness, bitterness, loneliness, and boredom. Behind the Max Factor facade of the happy homemaker, there is the reality of unkempt mothers who have spent the hours of their day consuming pills, whiskey, and the latest episode of the soap operas. There aren't any cookies; indeed, the children had to make their own breakfasts. That modern technology has benefitted the housewife is surely beyond question, and yet the release from much of the drudgery, the mutilating routine, and repetition of housework has left housewives with little to occupy their time and give meaning and purpose to their lives.

Most feminists devoutly insist that male theologians, in an attempt to develop an ideal or model for Christian women, have cultivated the notion that females are inferior to men, a kind of subspecies needing discipline and subordination. Women represented carnality, sexuality, sin, and evil. Eve was, after all, the temptress. Sacred scripture, the Fathers, and tradition have used the Genesis scenario relentlessly. Women have only been able to wail in agony over the truth of the representation—God, is this, can this be so?

The same philosophical tradition that defined men by attributes of mind and reason went on to determine women by their sexuality, and specifically, their wombs. The calling to be wife and mother was the true, the ultimate, the divinely ordained calling of woman. Moreover, since both masculine and feminine roles were God given, any attempt to change them was censured as rebellious and irreligious. When the European universities opened their doors in the 13th century, only men were permitted to enter. It was argued that formal education would serve no useful purpose for women, who were destined for the hearth.

Women who know that the Barbie Doll model for contemporary women is obscene have disclaimed it just as stridently as they disclaim the misogynist image of women gleaned from even the most perfunctory reading of the Wisdom literature of the Old Testament, and the definition of women advanced by the Church Fathers. "You are the devil's gateway," Tertullian told women. "How easily you destroyed man, the image of God. Because of the death which you brought upon us, even the Son of God had to die."

Women understand only too well the dreadful consequences of what has happened to them as the result of the judgment of the male having been metamorphosed into God's judgment. It then becomes the religious duty of women to take upon themselves the burden of guilt.

Patriarchal religion saw woman as a sex object, a nonperson to be used for procreative purposes or, narcissistically, for carnal pleasure. Sister Albertus Magnus McGrath summarizes the Old Testament thinking about women in the starkest terms.

> Nowhere is there any sense of the woman as person. She is property, a sexual object to be used and abused. Property of her father until adolescence, she is bargained away by him to a husband as soon as she becomes capable of bearing children. Like the slave, the wife addresses the husband as "ba'al" (master) or "adon" (lord).

A few women do find their way into the Old Testament as real persons, and they are stunning exceptions to the typological image of women as temptress, insatiable harlot, a nagging, garrulous wife. It is hard to imagine that the ideal wife of Proverbs 31:10-31 thought of herself as a possession of her husband. She is described in terms that many a "valiant" superwoman of the eighties can understand. The destructive image, however, is the one that dominates the sources. The account of the male sanction of the sexual abuse of women as found in Judges 19:22-30 is as abhorrent as any passage in literature.

Rosemary Ruether finds that in the writings of the Church Fathers the basic images of women are as whore, as wife, and as virgin.

> As whore, woman represents sinful carnality which is the essence of the fall. Here, woman is depicted as the bold strumpet, strutting forth in all her natural and artificial allures. Here, woman incarnates the very character of the sensual principle in revolt against its "head," and subverts the right ordering between mind and senses.

Ruether goes on to state that woman as wife was continually defined as an obedient and submissive body. Good wives cultivated an attitude of "total servility and meekness, even under harsh and unjust treatment." The wife had no rights and no choices; she had no autonomous dignity as a person. And, if the wife listened to

Augustine, she should not experience any pleasure in her sexuality, but "submit her body solely as an instrument for procreation."

The church has long been an accomplice, along with other powers in society, in the promotion and sustenance of this image of women. Freud encapsulated the concept in three words: "Anatomy is destiny." There are those who will find in this teaching good cause for his canonization.

From Paul's injunction that women should be silent in church, and keep her hair covered, the church has effectively gagged women for centuries. With equal adroitness, a male hierarchy has squelched those who suggested that more opportunities for creative contributions by women in the church need to be explored. Other than washing linen, arranging the altar flowers, scrubbing the sanctuary floor, cooking and serving the redundant chicken dinner, and, if a woman was really pushy, teaching third grade in CCD, little imagination has been expended on the married woman's role in a parish. After all, as one priest said, "someone has to do the dishes."

Clerics have assumed that married women know how to babysit, cook, clean, and sew, and not much else. Father Mosshamer, writing to priests and seminarians, tells them what a great joy it is for women to be of service, taking care of everything around the altar, decorating and cleaning, furnishing the pastor's vestments. "One can also notice," he says, "that the work is done out of love and not for pay."

The myriad demands made upon women by churchmen have been demeaning and insensitive. They have used their "alter Christus" status to seduce even gifted women into serving the church by catering to its clergy. Jesus approved of servanthood and he "emptied himself," but he did not practice hierarchy, and he did not defer. The dishes do have to be done. Feminists do not deplore servanthood, only its imbalance.

The ancient calendar of the saints has a rich assortment of categories for canonization, and the pious hagiographies that go with them. Holy women who were married, but not widows, find no special slot. Marriage may, and usually does, call for heroic virtues and deeds; perhaps it has demanded its own form of martyrdom. The general devaluation of both marriage and women by the church, however, does not permit the recognition in a formal way of this means of sanctification.

When the theologians speak of the virtues necessary for a good marriage — generosity, patience, forgiveness — they speak truly, as anyone who has happily celebrated several wedding anniversaries can attest. There can be no argument about the commendability of these virtues; what is faulty is the way women have been encouraged to act them out.

Generous women have typed their husband's term papers, but never their own.

Generous women have labored to keep his business accounts, although their own degree was in clinical nursing.

Generous women have hung clothes on the line so that he could have a golf cart before they purchased a dryer.

Patient women have endured sexual advances that were rough and bruising.

Patient women have waited for dinner and the ring of the phone.

They have sat through long nights as nurse, scrubbed floors and toilets, picked up wet towels and dirty socks, and packed endless miles of bologna sandwiches.

And forgiving women? Women, like God, have forgiven everything.

Women saints have portrayed the fortitude and fidelity of Mary's classic exemplar of Christian womanhood from the infancy of the church to the present time. They have excelled in callings as diversified as the militant Joan of Arc, the businesswoman Lydia of Philippi, the poetess Hilda, the mystic Margaret Mary. The Hungarian Queen Elizabeth fed the poor, Catherine of Siena advised the papacy, the great reformer Teresa of Avila reworked the rule and spirit of Carmel. We read of Priscilla who housed Paul and made tents, and the bustling administrator Mother Cabrini, and the young Clare, lifting the monstrance in the face of invading armies. They are all models, and come from a tradition that asserts that all persons are called to sainthood.

Elizabeth Schussler-Fiorenza finds the study of such women a liberating experience.

Any Catholic girl who grows up reading the "lives of the saints" might internalize all kinds of sexual hangups, but she would not think that her only vocation and her genuine

Christian call consists in being married and having children. Granted, from a theological and hagiographical point of view, the life choices of the women saints were often limited and conformed to male stereotypes. Yet they still contradicted the middle class cultural message that woman's Christian vocation demands the sacrifice of one's life for the career of a husband and the total dedication of one's time to diapering babies and decorating the living room.

The award of the Nobel Prize to Mother Teresa of Calcutta in 1979 was an appropriate recognition of a gallant woman, unconcerned with the ingrained cultural mores and images of women. But American women have not left their homes in droves to reach the hovels of India in order to become, like her; they do not even seem intent on the reform of the ghettos that scar most American cities.

American women are pleased that their sister Elizabeth Bayley Seton was the first native-born saint, but women are leaving convents more frequently than they are entering. The ought-to-be of these women saints does not seem to have much to say to American women who tend to identify with Mary Tyler Moore.

Suzanne Sommers, formerly of the cast of "Three's Company," remembers that before she was pictured as the centerfold of *Playboy*, she was cast as the madonna in her parochial school Christmas plays. Mary needed to be portrayed by someone demure, sweet, and pretty. No fatties, no buckteeth-and-glasses girls need apply. The subtle message was there. No matter how vehemently the holy nuns protested the evils of vanity, the fourth grade knew that only the slim, the lovely, the graceful were fit to stand in the role of the Mother of God. Janis Ian may have learned the truth "At Seventeen"; these girls grasped it much earlier.

Perhaps the sterling examples of many holy women are fragmented or lost in the harsh and brooding realization of the indignities women generally have experienced from the church. Pope Paul's repeated greeting to the faithful of both sexes gathered in Yankee Stadium in 1965, "Brothers and sons! Brothers and sons!" spoke volumes of discrimination that women will not quickly forget.

The bishops of Vatican II recognized that women are now finally active in "almost every area of life. It is appropriate that they should be able to assume their proper role in accordance with their nature. Everyone should acknowledge and favor the proper and necessary participation of women in cultural life." When women read the phrase "almost every area," they know that the exception is the church.

Mary Tyler Moore was mentioned earlier regarding a recent survey of young women of high school age who indicated that she was their ideal. Beverly Sills, Jessica Savich, Congresswoman Barbara Milkuski, the late Governor Ella Grasso, Helen Taussig, M.D., Gloria Steinem, and Supreme Court Justice Sandra O'Connor—all have significant achievements in their chosen professions, and may be considered worthy of emulation. In this same generation, the church still consigns inferior roles to women. Tissa Balysurya writes:

> The subordination of women to an inferior position is dehumanizing and unjust, and this cannot be the will of God. What was perhaps normal in the time of the Jews and Romans cannot be regarded as universally valid, particularly today when we have women Prime Ministers, legislators, Everest climbers, scientists, etc. . . . There seems hardly anything so manly in the ecclesiastical offices that a woman cannot perform. . . . If a woman is capable of being Prime Minister, there is no reason she cannot look after a diocese.

The Council Fathers who deliberately excluded women from any kind of active participation in their deliberations were no better than the secular society that has

> primed the young fillies to run fast, and then put impossible hurdles in their way. We tell young women that they are free to embark on careers, and then make it impossible for them to succeed in them. We tell them that they may have access to all the privileges and prerogatives of professionals, and then punish them if they accept the challenge. More important still, we put an enormous premium on their getting married, but make them pay an unconscionable price for falling in with our expectations. We blame them no matter what they do—refuse to run, kick over the traces, run wild, or become inert.

In other words, we lie.

The homemaker model, the traditional wife-mother model clearly has value, and generally feminists are protective of it, carefully respecting those who choose and find satisfaction in that role.

The human needs for meaning and belongingness, for security, for intimacy, the need to both give and receive of a joyous, tender love is satisfied in this intrinsic style of marriage. Milton Mayerhoff writes, "Through caring for certain others, by serving them through caring, a woman lives the meaning of her own life. In the sense in which a woman can ever be said to be at home in the world, she is at home not through dominating, or explaining, or appreciating, but through caring and being cared for." Even aggressive professional women have serious reservations about abandoning this role for the head-on pursuit of a career, particularly when their children are very young.

This model is not, however, a universally valid standard. Divisiveness occurs when women discuss the idealization of this role. Family traditions in regard to the homemaker exemplar differ widely among social, economic, ethnic, and racial groups. An individual's education, her reading, her experience, her observations of the marriages of other women, and particularly the quality of the marriage of her mother, will necessarily color her perception of the traditional role.

And women are talking. Some are saying that they will no longer accept that role either temporarily or for the duration of the marriage. Women no longer express their thinking about their marriages, and about marriage in general, in the discreet privacy of the friend's kitchen. Consciousness-raising groups all over the country have come into being, and women recognize and verbalize their perception of the fundamental vacuity of the position of housewife, and particularly the suburban housewife.

Many colleges now have outreach programs designed especially for women, with special courses for those who have been away from formal study for several years. These programs are attracting a wide and a very successful audience. They are a pleasure to have in class.

At the same time, feminist scholarship has come out of the academic halls, and best-selling books such as Nancy Friday's *My Mother, My Self* and Marilyn French's novel, *The Women's Room*, rest on suburban coffee tables. Clubs and organizations that used to be concerned with floral decorations and fashion shows now discuss the feminist concerns of such books. Marilyn French, for all her anger, evokes nods of assent. Yes, women say, yes. That is how it is.

Philip Slater suggests the frequent "jovial references to the multiplicity of roles played by housewives in our society serve to mask the fact that the housewife is a nobody." Clerical drivel about the meekness, humility, and sublime resignation of Mary to the will of God, and the annual sermon celebrating the raptures of motherhood are falling on deaf ears. For centuries the church has lauded the mother of God for these virtues, and in all propriety. Perhaps now is the time to make a case for Mary and other courageous wives and mothers as self-actualizers.

Kindregen notes with some validity: "Our society must accept the fact that the modern woman will reevaluate her role in society so that the old forms will not be an incomprehensible burden to her. She will no longer accept a secondary role in the Church, a second-best fatalism in the business world, or a destruction of her person in marriage." Married women will not live in a savage sacrament.

The formulas and dogmas that were useful to an older theology no longer fit the facts. Society has already recognized that marriage is in a state of transition, and that familial institutions as well as the role of women may be attacked or defended with equal vehemence.

Marc Poster, in his outline of various theories of the family, says, "It is blamed for oppressing women, abusing children, spreading neurosis and preventing community. It is praised for upholding morality, preventing crime, maintaining order and perpetuating civilization." Recognizing these aspects of marriage that may be blameworthy does not mean that women do not and will not have an immense investment in the values of marriage and the way it functions for them. It does mean that the concept of marriage, both as a sacrament and as an institution in the secular realm, need not be hardened or stabilized.

Women are more concerned than ever about the quality of marriage. They are equally concerned about finding a viable role model for themselves as married persons. Those who are serious about growth within their union will continue to cultivate the marital relationship with an arduous seeking to make it a living relationship of love. They know that marriage is a delicate, hard-working flower.

American women struggle now to remind themselves that they need not be victims of their cultural conditioning, and that women can create a new self and a new model in the light of a richer history than they know they have.

Today's women need to learn from the experiences and knowledge of their foremothers. They need to discover heroines.

Saint Luke (10:38-42) gives an account of Jesus and a visit he made to the house of Mary and Martha in Bethany. "Distracted with all the serving," Martha was annoyed that her sister had left her to do it alone. She complained to Jesus and petitioned him to speak to Mary, who was sitting and listening to him, that she would help.

Jesus did not respond to Martha's demand in the manner she had probably expected, but instead made the observation that Martha was "anxious and troubled about many things," while Mary had chosen the one thing necessary, the "better part." He had no intention of taking this from Mary. Jesus affirmed Mary.

Paul Tillich recognized the power of these few words when he commented that "the words Jesus speaks to Martha belong to the most famous of all the words in the Bible." The words used to belong to the exegetes who employed them to demonstrate the superiority of the contemplative over the active life. They now belong to women. The text graphically illustrates the dilemma that grips American women.

Robert Leslie comments:

> It could be said of Mary that she refused to be cast into the commonly accepted cultural model of homemaker. She insisted on being a person and not only a woman; she refused to fit into the stereotype which has been characterized as the feminine mystique.

The gospel incident anticipated the modern writers who complain about the dulling routine of the terrible treadmill that caretaking and nurturing can mean if it is unrelieved. It is so trite we forget its significance. Jesus was not dominated by an outlook that ultimately confined and narrowed human possibilities.

Jesus loved Martha (John 11:5) and he gave her a kind of emancipation proclamantion. Leslie reminds us:

> The lot of women in ancient civilizations was one of heavy and drugging toil. Not scorning Martha's service to

him, Jesus yet would lighten her load and encourage her to seize the freedom to cultivate her gifts of mind and spirit. His loving rebuke chides not Martha so much as the system that burdened her.

What Jesus offered Martha was the freedom from cultural and biblical images of women that both cheapened and bonded them. He offered her an inclusive vision that sees the ultimate purpose of all creation as liberation and maturation and healing.

He offered her the power to be made new.

CHAPTER SEVEN

Toward a
Lived Theology of Marriage

And may you see your children's children. . . .

Psalm 128:6

ON THEIR GOLDEN WEDDING ANNIVERSARY THE FRAIL, OLD COUPLE
walked down the aisle of Sts. Simon and Jude Church in Bethlehem, Pennsylvania as if they had planned grey hair and grandchil-
dren. Three sons, two daughters, and their spouses waited at the
sanctuary railing with a young priest who was anxious to finish the
early morning Mass and get out on the golf course. The grandchil-
dren were there, fidgeting in their Sunday best, the easterners eye-
ing their California cousins who were virtual strangers. Twenty-
one of them, whose names read like a litany of the saints, clustered
around their parents.

81

Later in the day there would be a party — turkey and ham and a whole side of beef, cases of beer and gallons of bourbon and gin were ready for the onslaught of the brothers and sisters and their families, the whole clan from Philadelphia who held the ancient faith of Ireland and of Rome.

Her grandsons had presented Nana with an orchid corsage, and she wore diamond ear clips from an anniversary past. Pop-Pop wore a new suit, and all the bills were paid. The processional cross standing in the sanctuary carried a bronze plaque with their names on it. Organ music accompanied them down the white carpet usually reserved for brides, and Frances Margaret and Oscar Joseph knelt again to repeat solemnly the vows they had whispered half a century ago. "To have and to hold, from this day forward . . . until death. . . ." The bride had ripened into the golden richness of the woman.

When did it happen, their sacramental moment? Was it in fact during the 6:00 A.M. Nuptial Mass long ago when they hushed their promises into the stillness of early morning? Was it later that evening in some unknown room in Manayunk when they came together as husband and wife? Was it in the quiet moment when they cradled the gentleness of Marie? Was it one of the troubled times when their eyes met over the meager tables set during the lean, dark years of the depression? Was it when Joseph was ill with typhoid, or when Edward left for war? Was it the prideful day when Leon enrolled at the university, or the laughing day when Zita sang and danced in a minstrel show?

Nana always talked of breakfast and laundry; if grief existed, piles of soiled clothes existed, too. She rationed her depths and heights so they would last a long time.

The simplicity of her theology of marriage was not designed by the learned scholars whose legal Latin terms she could not understand. Hers was a theology of caring promises, a theology of make do, of gratitude, a theology of enough.

Her faith in her husband and their marriage was uncluttered with appliances, cosmetics, or designer clothes. The innumerable assortment of pills, jellies, foams, and other contraceptive devices were foreign to her way of life. The easy assurance that abortion was possible should the devices fail was unspeakable. One did not terminate a pregnancy unnaturally. One did not terminate a marriage.

The national cult of Miss America never touched her. She was not sophisticated, bored, well-read, alcoholic, addicted to valium, or forgetful of God. Hers was not a frenetic search for career or club. She stirred the jam, chose a dress, visited a friend, prayed her rosary, scolded a child. Solid in her marriage, she achieved new relationships, accepting into her life and caring the men and women her children came to love, and their children and their loves, and their children "unto the fourth generation."

"Marriage and the family," Anthony Padovano says, "is the most effective sign we have of the relationship between life, faith and love." This marriage was indeed such a sign. It was a revelatory event, and, therefore, a true sacrament.

In a very real way, the simple story of the marriage that became the life of this woman is comparable to the story of the strength and toughness and practicality that are important segments of the life of the mother of God, who was also the wife of Joseph the carpenter. Self-confidence and independence were among Mary's virtues, though they are never sung in her litanies. She knew how to make good use of joy; when pleasure came, she called it by its spare and proper name.

Mary, like marriage, has been given over to the sentimentalists, who present her as innocent, pure, and protected. The evangelists did not see her exclusively that way, and it is difficult to believe that Jesus, who had an immense respect for her freedom, did either.

A valiant woman, she is called Tower of Ivory, House of Gold, and of course she was, if there is any poetry left to see. The lyric girl of the Magnificat, yes, but Mary was also a practical woman of her own time, and she had to find herself in dynamic relationship to the world of Nazareth, Egypt, and Jerusalem. There was a slashing directness in her remark to her son, "They have no wine."

The realization must never be lost that it was as true for Mary as it was for Nana, and as it is for the modern feminist: a woman is what she does with her freedom. Mary had to grow in her own consciousness as a woman, a wife, and a mother, a mother with a rebel son. The function of every person, even the holy ones, is to live. Unused freedom in any life renders it little different from enslavement.

Much of what Mary had to do, as she pondered in her heart the ways she must be alive for God, did not differ at all from the task of Nana in her own time, or the work of contemporary feminists. All women need to set the many values of this world — careers, relationships, cosmetics, appliances, play, children, love, freedom — into an integrated perspective, and see all of them in their verity and sacramentality. It is the work of a lifetime.

Jesus himself learned from the nursery of his mother's love. From the gospel that Mary is, women have learned that the clarity and authenticity of themselves as persons come only when they consciously seek to understand and experience and then extend the human capacity to love.

The sacramentality of Mary as perceived by contemporary women lies not in the idealization or the fantasy of her as the sweet, slender child-bride untouched by sin, raising up her immaculate hands that hold the perfect child. This bland and monolithic image has been replaced by one that transcends standardization. Mary did not wilt at the annunciation, or at the crucifixion either. She stood.

The drama of her life and the sacrament of her marriage to Joseph were not devoid of the savage. No life, no marriage is. The recorded doubt of her betrothed husband, the laborious journey to Bethlehem and subsequent flight into Egypt are storied examples. "And a sword will pierce through your own soul," was the cruel warning of Simeon (Luke 2:35).

There was the devastation when the child was lost, only to be followed by the curtness of his response after his parents located him. And in a few years, the death of Joseph robbed her of his support and strength. The stories of this holiest of women are few, but crucial enough to illustrate her commonality with all women in all times.

When was the sacramental moment of her marriage? Was it at the moment of their betrothal? Was it when she understood that Joseph accepted the miracle that was growing in her womb? Was it in Bethlehem, when together they beheld the living God, born of her flesh and given into his keeping? Was it when they clung to each other, utterly confused, and watched the tableau of Jesus confounding the teachers? Was it sometime, a rare moment of the hidden years of ardent chastity when they waited on the will of God?

Did she not close his eyes in death, her Joseph's eyes, and did not her veil cover their final kiss? Was it then?

The stories of two women and their personal experience of marriage is never enough. Every woman and every marriage is unique, and yet marriage and women have been governed as if they were not.

Mary has always been a problem for the theologians. The Council of Ephesus victoriously proclaimed her "theotokos," but the title came at the expense of prolonged controversy with Nestorious. Protestants have shied away from her veneration in a divisive manner, claiming that Catholic devotion to the mother of God was in reality adoration. The churchmen have mythologized her beyond belief, and they have ignored her without excuse.

All women have been, in general, a problem for both philosophers and theologians. Throughout the ages, both groups have been consistent in their denigration of women. Plato, Aristotle, Origen, Tertullian, Jerome, Aquinas, Luther, Calvin, Kant, Hegel, Schopenhauer, Nietzsche, Meredith, and Wylie have all contributed to a pervasive and essentially negative view of women (not to mention Saint Paul and Hugh Hefner).

Freud himself wondered what women wanted, and after a generation or two of extensive studies of developmental patterns, and male and female differences, Robert May is constrained to write: "Our sore need is for a language and space in which to talk about the distinguishing characteristics of men and women without being demeaning to either."

Students of contemporary society worry that women have become too dominant, and even women writers like Ellen Peck nervously observe that *A Funny Thing Happened on the Way to Equality*. The question of women raises difficulties in the courts, at the polls, and in the labor market. Medical research and legal reform have felt the stampede for women's liberation. Affirmative action groups are on the college campuses. And now the church, the last bastion of male dominance, must face the searing problem of women, and the issues raised by women in reference to sacramental marriage.

Edward Schillebeeckx has observed: "When the Church found herself in almost total jurisdictional control of matrimonial affairs, she discovered it was a highly complex issue." Because marriage is a common, social event, it makes sense to people in a secular way in which some of the other sacraments — eucharist, confirmation, ordination, for example — do not. All of these special signs, Monika Hellwig explains, "have to be interpreted in the tradition to be understood. The ceremony of marriage, the mutual self-giving of two people, does not need any explanation as the coming through water or the imposition of hands needs explanation."

The history of sacramental marriage has evolved alongside the herstory of women; though permanent, the sacrament is always in process. Any tradition that seeks to interpret the sacrament necessarily includes in its interpretation its own peculiar vision of women. Schillebeeckx has shown that the pattern of marriage at any given time and place is the result of many different ideas and social factors. The church is inexorably bound up with culture.

The structure of society in the Middle Ages allowed little mention of real happiness and emotional satisfaction as a goal of the conjugal relationship. A man's mistress or his concubines provided for those needs. Marriage then was essentially a business contract made to enhance political and military alliances for the wealthy and powerful, and to offer economic security, children, and relief from sexual tension for the poor.

The modern bride would find it inconceivable that her suitor and her father would haggle over her "price," and that she, as an ideal Christian wife, would be expected "to submit humbly to her lord, raise his bastards if he so desired, never utter a word of disapproval, and by earnest efforts of love try to win him back from distracting influences."

In the face of such savagery, some theologians are fond of assuring women that their position in society was improved by the advent of Christian faith and times. They attempt to placate feminists who rage against the blatantly sexist language in scripture and many formal prayers of the church by reminding them that the sacred writers were simply reflecting the attitudes of the societies in which they lived. That may be true enough, but what is frequently omitted in their arguments is the record of the church that not only absorbed those attitudes, but practiced and even recommended them. In pious homilies, for example, men "were exhorted from the pulpit to beat their wives and wives to kiss the rod that beat them." It is doubtful that any living American priest has ever said that from his pulpit, a definite improvement.

The Council of Trent defined the sacrament of marriage in the 16th century; we are approaching the 21st. It took many, too many, centuries for the order of society to move from the concept of women as vassals, as chattel, as domesticated animals, even as unworthy of eternal life, to the concept of the ideal Christian wife in American society. No longer considered the property of her husband, now she is the one who will provide emotional closeness, who will share similar intellectual and spiritual values. She expects the new covenant she makes "to embrace the whole person of both partners in all their dimensions," as Walter Kasper explains it. Marriage is democratic now; it is for the mature, the adult. It is for equals.

In almost every reading of American spirituality relevant to marriage an expectation of a covenant is expressed, a counterdefinition of the contract order of marriage. Women talk about sharing and intimacy and personal dignity, and a kind of happiness that has little to do with having. Commitment takes precedence over romantic love.

Daniel DiDomizio's insight reads:

> Two persons, who have discerned that their lives are converging, encounter God's presence as they progress towards an intimacy which is expressed in a total response to each other, emotional, spiritual and genital. This intertwining of two lives that evolves only through the passage of years is the sacrament of marriage. It is both a commitment and an ongoing process. We are married and yet we are always marrying.

Intimacy refers to enduring ability, a strong virtue, that enables a person to commit herself to and effectively care for the significant others in her life. Intimacy is the contemporary phrasing or restatement of the evocative image of Genesis 2:24, "A man leaves his father and his mother and cleaves to his wife and they become one flesh."

The virtue of Christian intimacy is refined and developed through all the joys and struggles of married life. Evelyn and James Whitehead write, "In many different situations of family life we feel the invitation and challenge of intimacy: how to make our being together . . . work to bring us even closer, to make our love for each other grow."

Intimacy demands equality, the equality of two whole persons coming together. It is a life-task of sharing that is not merely physical, but also psychological. "A happy couple give to each other out of the abundance of their maturity," priest-poet J. Joseph Gallagher writes. There is a kind of whole knowledge in this thought.

When marriage was viewed primarily as a contract, almost a business arrangement, the theologians of that time naturally spoke of the sacramental moment as happening when the couple formally agreed (consensus) to be united in a legal and sacral bond. The husband at that moment became the "head of the household," and the wife submitted herself without question to his will. Equality was never a consideration, and the good wife "did her duty." Conjugal rights and duties were spelled out with some precision. One woman remembered confessing that she and her husband had slept in separate bedrooms once when he had the flu. She was reprimanded and told that the fourth commandment required their perpetual cohabitation in bed and board. The fourth?

Another time in history when marriage was considered primarily as the institution that best served the process of founding and sustaining a family on earth, as well as populating heaven, the theologians argued that the marital union that had been consummated by sexual intercourse could never be dissolved. In other words, the sacramental moment was fixed at the time of the physical consummation.

This debate reflects the almost obsessional interest the church has had in focusing on and fixing the precise locus of the sacrament. Legally precise definition was obligatory for theologians trained in the tradition of canon and Roman law.

There have always been norms regulating the exercise of sexuality, and they are enormously convenient for the canon lawyer, the tribunal officials, and the pastor. Marriage and the family cannot be regarded as a purely private matter. They are social, public, and in a wide sense, political. At one time or another, this legal stance of regulation has curtailed some matrimonial abuses. As Rosemary Haughton points out: "You can't oblige people to love one another, but you can see that their union conforms to ascertainable norms."

This legalistic understanding of marriage that stressed conjugal rights and duties, and emphasized the ritual moment as the transition into the married state, is woefully inadequate for those who wish to view marriage as a "religious passage of intimacy." Theologians have not been eager to explore this concept of definition because, as the Whiteheads claim, they are fearful of an anthropological reductionism that "explains away the uniqueness of the sacraments." It might also reduce the power of churchmen to control marriage.

When a couple chooses to live together in sacramental marriage, and fulfills all the diocesan requirements, which include civil forms and license, this is an issue of the form of the relationship. It does not and cannot reveal how the man and the woman will relate to one another. Successful and happy marriages may be what the sociologists describe as intrinsic unions, with the couple valuing and needing the physical and psychological proximity of the other, or the marriage may be the less personal but utilitarian union. In any case, this is a question not of form, but of process.

The human experience of contemporary marriage for couples intent upon avoiding the unnecessary legalisms and savage aspects of their sacramental union, and creating a loving bond that duly honors equality and personal growth, has literally forced the theologians to overstep the juridical abstractions and walk into the reality itself. Peter Berger warns:

> To go against the order of society is always to risk plunging into anomy. To go against the order of society as religiously legitimated, however, is to make a compact with the primeval forces of darkness. To deny reality as it has been socially defined is to risk falling into irreality, because it is well nigh impossible in the long run to keep up alone and without social support one's own counterdefinition of the world.

Modern couples find that the process of marriage must be grounded in reality, their own reality, and this means that marriage must always be considered in a fresh and creative light. "It is not the theologians and the philosophers who have posed the problem," Von Gagern says. "It is life itself." No matter how elegant the form and design of marriage, if the process is not appropriate, then the union will generate difficulties, if not atrocities. The sacramental ritual is certainly not magic.

Cultural anthropology has shown again and again the varieties of the form of marriage, as well as its process. Some cultures recognize marriages quite dissimilar to the Western norm of marriage as an irrevocable contract made at a particular time in absolute formality and finality. Present attempts to preserve the ascertainable norms of the sacrament mean that it is "harder to get married in Church," as Sister Mary Ann Walsh reports in her account of those marriage preparation programs that are now functioning.

Bishop J. Francis Stafford of the Baltimore Archdiocese and Chairman of the U.S.C.C. Commission on Marriage and the Family agrees. He decries the high incidence of interfaith marriages in the United States, the highest in the world, and recognizes that "the deepest challenge of catechesis is in formational programs for those about to be married." One can only hope that the formational programs are not simply another case of too little, too late. The bishop speaks of norms at a time when women are becoming more sensitive to the ideology of process, and distrustful of clerical authority as it governs many aspects of their lives.

Marriage preparation programs are in their infancy, and there is a wide range of requirements an engaged couple must satisfy before a particular diocese will permit their reception of the sacrament. All the dioceses are legitimately concerned that the sacrament in its purity be protected from the secular and materialistic inroads of contemporary life and thought with all its functional character. Schillebeeckx correctly observes that the tasks and skills of modern marriage require outside help more than ever before.

> It is not so much that a new pattern of married and family life has been created, but rather that every married person and each family realizes that there is a task to be accomplished. What each marriage has to do is to establish its own pattern of married life, building this up on a foundation of the inspirational force of an inner conviction and an inner plan of life.

Feminists may very well agree that help from the church and its social services needs to be forthcoming for those approaching a modern marriage. Feminists are not antimarriage, and they want couples to have happiness, peace, and fulfillment. They express, however, little certainty that the church's image of women as happy housewife and fruitful mother is truly past tense, and that the church's "help" is not just another bandaid to cover the gaping wound of the devaluation of the lives and purposes of women, married and otherwise.

There are far too many selfish and morally retarded men and women tinkering with the marriage "game"—boys and girls really—who need the emphatic telling that marriage is not a casual relationship and raising children is a sober business. Sex is rarely a domestic pet.

There are many couples in their late teens and early twenties who are not sufficiently wise and mature to make the binding, permanent choice that is a sacrament, a choice that must be preserved over a lifetime that may extend over a period of some 50 or even 70 years. Priestly reluctance to preside at such unions of the very young is well founded.

If it has become more difficult to marry in the church, then the authorities appear to have backed themselves into the position of having to give some form or recognition to a form of nonsacramental marriage, perhaps as a kind of dress rehearsal for the real thing. The very immature who have never experienced the total giving of self in human love are not likely to listen when theologians like Dominian tell them that the husband-wife relationship "begins on the cross and never leaves it if it is to remain a genuine imitation of the Christ/Church one." Perhaps all they want or are capable of is what sounds like half-a-marriage. (Why does "slight case of cancer" come to mind?) Such recognition may be unprecedented, but it is unquestionably true that the church has bent the gospel on some of the other "hard sayings" of Jesus. We attach too long a penalty.

Nana had a traditional marriage, and it worked. In addition, it was an inspirational force. (My own mother's marriage was anything but ordinary. She was married at 44 and widowed a decade later when my father was 75. I retain only a child's sense of a peaceful home, a lively father and a serene mother.) I would be surprised if my mother, my mother-in-law, and a million women like them ever averted to the rich symbolism that the biblical writers have invested in the marital relationship as sacrament. It is doubtful that they ever worried much about self-fulfillment or peak experiences or passages of intimacy. The immediacy of those women's experience was the solitary knowledge that if they wished to marry, they must marry in the church or live in sin. It was yesterday's knowledge; it is today's.

But women know that all Christian marriages are *not* holy unions; many are nothing more than endurance contests, or gelid facades. Women know that the really savage marriages are not sacred signs of anything. They are lies.

As responsible and intelligent human beings, women ask if it is not easily discernible that while tragedy and serious illness unite some families, they divide others?

Is it, in fact, true that conjugal love can die, does die?

What does "in the Lord" really mean?

Might it be more accurate to claim that some marriages fail because the sacramental moment never occurred in the first place?

And the most fundamental question: how is the truly loving marriage in Christ radically different from a thoroughly secularized but equally caring relationship?

Give us more than tired answers, women ask.

If it could be argued that marriage becomes sacramental not at the ceremony, and not during the initial act of intercourse as older theologies have said, but at some, perhaps indefinable time, a moment over the process of the long years that the union endured, would not the living reality of the symbol have more meaning? "The sacrament," Dinter says, "adheres in the relationship itself, not only in the vowing of that relationship in a public ceremony."

Women seem to understand this clearly, though none has articulated it on a theological level. Part of the genius of women is that they are always aware of the wonderful and painful blendings of life, and the profound processes of growth. Elizabeth Janeway in *Powers of the Weak* illustrates:

> She has witnessed and participated in a long slow process of growth and learning that has demanded a continual interaction with her own being. Some part of her knows, whether she can articulate it or not, that abstractions and obiter dicta don't always—don't often perhaps—fit individual situations, and that the options life offers are not confined to either/or dichotomies.

The price of process is always some kind of loss. The loss here is of a theology that is abstract, organized, and structured. The redefinition of marriage as process involves a commitment that is like no other because it is open-ended. Thus, Richard Conklin writes:

> That is why those who get married know not what they do, know not where the relationship will end. And that is

why no preparation is adequate to the demands marriage imposes, even as family, church and state are constrained to try. One is tempted to offer the advice medieval cartographers put on the edge of their flat world. Out there are dragons.

The programs geared to assist young couples as they prepare for marriage need creativity and courage if they are to meet the dragons. Marriage is the richness of life, and its silent desert, too. But in any case, it is not a disembodied argument. If the sacrament of marriage doesn't have to do with women's lives, what does it encompass?

Programs and people, including feminist people, still see permanent marriage as an ideal, whatever dragons must be met and vanquished to attain it. Columnist Ellen Goodman says: "People talk about lifetime marriages with a kind of longing, and wonder. And hunger." My husband kissed me good morning today for the ten thousand, five hundred and eighty-fifth time. That's special!

Good and holy marriages do exist and their stories are fertile and beautifully useful as paradigms. The abundant grace of God's action, promised by the sacrament, however real it may be, seems clouded by the reality of life for many women, just as the definition that the consensus constitutes the sacramental moment, however true, is only part of the truth. There is simply no point in telling the stories of Mary, of Nana, of myriads of women of past generations whose marriages were holy and happy, unless the memory and recognition that some marriages are savage is kept alive.

Holy marriages, happy marriages are very personal, incapable of verification and objective measurement. The whole cloth is a fabric woven of many fibers and in intricate patterns that often have no clearly defined framework. The legitimate concerns of free women must be worked into the cloth; that is a prime feminist concern. "If feminism means anything, it means we can and must dream our dreams and that these dreams, in the final analysis, must unite us, in peace and fellowship, with other human beings rather than divide us, one from another."

A new thinking about sacramental marriage involves the risk of human error, and also the enormous risk of losing or weakening faith. It must be done, because faith is not something you lose, it is something you cease to shape your life by. "The very future of women in religion," McBride writes, "depends upon whether we can exorcise our male bias from our beliefs and whether we can admit that human nature is constantly being shaped by new insights and new forces." Alfred North Whitehead promises, "Religions commit suicide when they find their inspirations in their dogmas."

Women are concerned with the quality of the marriages that do survive. "The value of a marriage is to be gauged by the joy it affords, not by its longevity," psychologist Nathanael Branden writes. "There is nothing admirable about two people remaining together in marriage, thoroughly frustrated and miserable, for fifty years."

In a stacatto summary, Jean Stapleton writes:

> Loveless marriages may die out, and they should. Neurotic, game-playing marriages may die out and should. Marriage for money and status may die out and should. Marriage as a device for allowing half-persons to survive may die out and should. Marriage for sex alone is already dead. . . .

So the ultimate challenge of theology and women is to become allies with the process of understanding and longing, the process of growth and inevitable change, respecting tradition and the call of the future. The dialogue to meet this challenge has only begun; hopefully, it will not be stillborn.

Sacramental marriage between a man and a woman, equals in covenant made in the Lord, does not die. Such a conjugal union, in which there is no savagery, is a great mystery.

And therefore the wisdom of women must here keep silence.

Epilogue

IT HAS BEEN ALMOST A DECADE SINCE I BEGAN TO WONDER WHAT WOULD happen if anyone attempted a synthesis of the theologians and the feminists on Christian marriage. If I have learned anything during this time, it is that they do not dialogue very well. They duel.

I have this fantasy of Dr. Mary Daly and the Sovereign Pontiff as the principals, each dressed in black trousers and white ruffled shirts with stock collars. Their seconds on this misty morning are Rosemary Ruether and the Apostolic Delegate, who insisted on wearing his red. Daly has had a good stiff belt of Simone de Beauvoir, and the Pope has swallowed the misogynist writings of Saint Jerome whole. They count off twenty paces, and turn to fire the pistols. When the smoke clears, _____ lies in the dust. There are no duellos.

Marriage will survive American feminism, and so will the church. All three institutions have a high tolerance level for criticism, heresy, and desertion, as well as hatred, mockery, and the awful insolence of being ignored. But I do not want to speculate about endurance or survival, or even about which duellist leaves the contest arena in victory or in shame. The theology of marriage

95

is not about surviving or winning. It is about making alive, about the process of peace, and ultimately, it is about love.

I believe that living persons and vital institutions can be only if they become; they exist only if they can change. I say this even as I reverently applaud the church as the venerable custodian or guardian of truth; and I say it in anguish because I fear that the church, for feminists, may become janitor.

The church has modified its vision many times during its long history of becoming; the status of women has changed too. The shifts during the past decades have been both radical and rapid. Women who search for new values in this time have been disadvantaged because they were caught between the gelid rapiers of authoritarian, conservative, patriarchal teachings, and the not too finely honed darts of innovative but rebellious promoters of women's causes. There is simply no painless way of fusing dreams and reality.

The theology of marriage coming from papal and clerical authorities is still largely determined upon the preservation of an ideal, and preserving it by fear, law, and moral sanction. Few marriages of any ecclesial era could sustain the scrutiny of being compared to the sublime symbolism of marriage as found in Saint Paul. The theology written in this vein is more a theology of power than a theology of conjugal love.

It is the power that women resent and want to transform.

As a Christian feminist, I need to be convinced that churchmen are totally sincere and serious when they confront the many issues concerning women in the church, and that they are not eternally grounded in the sludge of the convenience of old values and older ideas. I need to know that they listen openly to what women say. I need to believe that their gestures of reconciliation come from internal conviction, and not from the pressures of expediency or economics.

The great legal minds that designed the system by which marriage has been defined and governed had a magnificent universal vision. Great pastoral minds can, indeed must, meld law and love into a new theology of marriage that is mindful of the process of women who live in a society that includes them in functions they were not commonly accorded in past centuries. What the theologians lose in power, they may gain in humanity.

And the feminists. They have so often and so relentlessly been relegated to the role of antagonist, seen as possessed of the disturbed mind of the heresiarch and the rebellious will of the unorthodox. Will they remain silent, angry, frustrated forever? Will they simply weary of the tensions engendered by their activism and its raw rejection, and finally withdraw, walking away like the rich young man, sad? What follows if they are not interested in a duel to the death?

We know that early Christianity did not own an absolute dogmatic formula. It was a continuum of ideas, and variations of doctrine were common, reflecting as they did the belief, the style of ordinary, simple people. Feminism has a right to be part of that continuum, part of the process, and in the last analysis, part of the doctrine.

It is well known that Pope John Paul II likes to ski. I wonder if he also dances. David danced in passion before the tabernacle of Yahweh. Jesus, himself Lord of the Dance, included it in his parable of the Prodigal Son. It has been said that he "danced" upon his savage cross.

Although the dance is festive movement, it is serious as well, for dancing is the symbol of the harmonious balance and exercise of all our higher qualities, in union with a central idea, an ideal of responsible relatedness.

There are many kinds of dances. Sometimes the orchestra plays the music of the gavotte, sometimes a waltz or a dirge. Sometimes it is the stylized, intricate movements of the minuet, or the wild, free expressions of modern choreography. The rhythm expands, circles, goes out and then returns; it includes the wider group of spectators who begin to clap or sway with the tempo, impatient to roll up the rug and dance themselves.

When you are skiing, the best part is coming down the slope. Similarly for some, dancing is a natural, spontaneous, intuitive rhythm. The elegance, the grace of others comes after discipline and practice. There is always the possibility that some klutz will step on a partner's toes doing a reel or a simple two-step. But only those who are afraid to dream are afraid to dance.

I have a dream of a holy dance. The dancers enter the stage from opposing wings. They are careful, tentative; they have not met before. Sure of his program, he must give up something of his own pride to be sensitive to her movements. Certain of her grace, she must surrender something of her doubts to trust in his strength. The dancers must accommodate each other, they must connect, they must interpret the music *together*. His timing must be accurate, she could be distracted, one or the other might fail to execute a move perfectly, but their combined creative energies complete and complement the score. In a way, they wed. The conductor has willed that it be so.

Unlike the duel, which ends in death or wound or empty "satisfaction," the dance ends in joy. Let us hope for that joy, that living connectedness that is truly redemptive, sealed by the spirit, in Christ Jesus our Lord.

Credo of a
Christian Feminist

Christian feminists believe in the Maternity of God, the Feminism of Jesus, and the Androgony of the Holy Spirit.

Christian women believe that God created all women as full human persons, equal in every respect with men, and that the redemptive act of Jesus Christ was inclusive of all womankind. They believe that the Spirit of God moving through the whole church encourages and inspires Christian feminism.

Women affirm that they are not to be defined simply by their biology and unique capacities for reproduction, but by the universal call to Christian witness and ministry and freedom.

Women believe that the God, who Saint John says is love, liberates them now for new possibilities and experiences, and they call for the cessation of sexist and archaic attitudes toward women in the church. They believe that a patriarchal authority that continues to condone and foster discrimination against women is in serious error. They experience discrimination as sin.

Women are profoundly committed to the ideals of Christian marriage and the values of fidelity and intimacy and love that abide in its richness. They intend to be generous, tender, and caring in the wonderful sharing of conjugal life. Their priorities lie in their self-giving and devotion to their husbands and children, but they believe that this is reasonable only in conjunction with the fullest development of themselves as persons with special capabilities, interests, and needs.

They believe that no woman should bring a child to life except by her free choice. True motherhood does not admit to coercion, it is not automatic, it is not essential, it is not innate.

Christian women subscribe to responsible parenthood, but not to the idea that every act of sexual intercourse must be entirely open to the possibility of new life. They do not accept the teaching that the use of artificial contraceptives is morally evil. They respect those women who choose to remain childless.

Feminists defend the dignity of the homemaker and the integrity of the women who invest in a career. They know that the great human act of sexuality should never be trivialized by either. They condemn pornography, rape, incest, and the exploitation of women by much of modern advertising. They are concerned about the wanton destructiveness that is abortion.

Women believe that the high incidence of conjugal crime can and must be changed, and they believe that the current gender arrangements are capable of modification.

Free Christian women believe in human life and human love sealed by the Spirit. They realize that women throughout history have been the prime transmitters of culture and of faith, and they know that all human life that touches theirs must be made holy in the touching.

They believe that the love that is their marriage, and then becomes new life and is nourished by their bodies, inspired by their minds, and cradled lovingly in their arms, will ultimately be taken up by the very arms of the Lord God.

And so it is.

Bibliography

Abbot, Walter M., S.J., general editor. *The Documents of Vatican II*. New York: Guild Press, 1966.

Barbeau, Clayton C. *Creative Marriage: The Middle Years*. New York: Seabury Press, 1976.

_____. ed. *Future of the Family*. New York: Bruce, 1971.

Bassett, William W., ed. *The Bond of Marriage: An Ecumenical and Interdisciplinary Study*. Notre Dame, IN: University of Notre Dame Press, 1968.

_____ and Peter Huizing, eds. *The Future of Christian Marriage*. New York: Herder and Herder, 1973.

Baum, Gregory. *Man Becoming*. New York: Herder, 1970.

Berger, Peter. *The Sacred Canopy*. Garden City, NY: Doubleday, 1967.

Bernard, Jessie. *The Future of Marriage*. Toronto: Bantam, 1972.

_____. *The Future of Motherhood*. New York: Dial Press, 1974.

Bertocci, Peter A. *Sex, Love and the Person*. Mission, KS: Sheed and Ward, 1967.

Bianchi, Eugene C. and Rosemary Radford Ruether. *From Machismo to Mutuality*. New York: Paulist Press, 1976.

Bier, William C., S.J., ed. *Marriage: A Psychological and Moral Approach*. New York: Columbia University Press, 1965.

Blank, Rubin and Gertrude Blank. *Marriage and Personal Development*. New York: Columbia University Press, 1968.

Bockle, Frans, ed. *The Future of Marriage as Institution.* New York: Herder and Herder, 1970.

Boff, Leonardo. *The Question of Faith in the Resurrection of Jesus.* Chicago: Franciscan Herald Press, 1972.

Boucher, M. "Some Unexplored Parallels to 1 Cor 11:11-12 and Gal 3:28: The New Testament Role of Women," *Catholic Biblical Quarterly* (Jan. 1969) pp. 50-58.

Branden, Nathanael. *The Psychology of Romantic Love.* Los Angeles: Tarcher, 1980.

Brieg, Joseph A. *The Mysteries of Marriage.* New York: Sheed and Ward, 1963.

Brinkley, Luther J. *Conflict of Ideals.* New York: Van Nostrand, 1969.

Bromiley, Geoffrey W. *God and Marriage.* Grand Rapids, MI: Eerdmans, 1980.

Brothers, Joyce. *Woman.* New York: MacFadden-Bartell, 1961.

Bruns, J. Edgar. *God as Woman, Woman as God.* New York: Paulist Press, 1975.

Burghardt, Walter, S.J., ed. *Woman: New Dimensions.* New York: Paulist Press, 1975.

Burke, T. W. *The Gold Ring, God's Perfect Plan for Marriage.* New York: McKay, 1963.

Burtchaell, James Tunstead, C.S.C., and others. *Marriage Among Christians.* Notre Dame, IN: Ave Maria Press, 1977.

Buytendijk, F. J. *Woman: A Contemporary View.* Glen Rock, NJ: Newman, 1968.

Byron, Brian. "1 Cor 7:10-15: A Basis for Future Catholic Discipline on Marriage and Divorce." *Theological Studies* 34 (May 1973) pp. 429-445.

Callahan, Sidney Cornelia. *Beyond Birth Control.* New York: Sheed and Ward, 1968.

Chodorow, Nancy. *The Reproduction of Mothering.* Berkeley: University of California Press, 1978.

Christ, Carol P. and Judith Plaskow, eds. *Womanspirit Rising.* San Francisco: Harper & Row, 1979.

Clark, Lorenne M. G. and Lynda Lange. *The Sexism of Social and Political Theory: Women and Reproduction from Plato to Nietzsche.* Toronto: University of Toronto Press, 1979.

Clark, Stephen B. *Man and Woman in Christ.* Ann Arbor, MI: Servant Books, 1980.

Cole, William Graham. *Sex and Love in the Bible.* London: Hodder and Stoughton, 1959.

Cox, Harvey. *The Seduction of the Spirit.* New York, New York: Simon and Schuster, 1973.

Cua, A. S. *Dimensions of Moral Creativity.* University Park, PA: Pennsylvania State University Press, 1978.

Curran, Charles E. *A New Look at Christian Morality.* Notre Dame, IN: Fides, 1970.

Daly, Mary. *Beyond God the Father.* Boston: Beacon Press, 1973.
_____. *Gyn/Ecology: The Metaethics of Radical Feminism.* Boston: Beacon Press, 1978.

Daniel-Rops, Henri. *Love Is Forever.* Dublin: Scepter, 1964.

Davidson, Terry. *Conjugal Crime.* New York: Ballantine Books, 1978.

De Beauvoir, Simone. *The Second Sex.* New York: Modern Library, 1968.

de Castillejo, Irene Claremont. *Knowing Woman: A Feminine Psychology.* New York: Harper & Row, 1973.

Di Domizio, Daniel. "Marriage: A Story and a Sacrament." *Catholic World* (1979) 222. pp. 255-258.

Dinnerstein, Dorothy. *The Mermaid and the Minotaur.* New York: Harper & Row, 1976.

Dinter, Paul E. "Pastoral Dilemmas with Marriage." *America* 142 (1980) 4. pp. 75-78.

Dominian, J. *Christian Marriage: The Challenge of Change.* London: Darton, Longman and Todd, 1967.

Douglas, Ann. *The Feminization of American Culture.* New York: Avon, 1977.

Dowling, Colette. *The Cinderella Complex.* New York: Summit, 1981.

Dreikurs, Rudolf, M.D. *The Challenge of Marriage.* New York: Hawthorne, 1946.

Elshtain, Jean Bethke. "A Feminist's Journey." *Commonweal* (June 5, 1981) pp. 331-333.

Elwood, J. Murray. *Growing Together in Marriage.* Notre Dame, IN: Ave Maria Press, 1977.

Freeman, Jo, ed. *Woman: A Feminist Perspective.* New York: Mayfield, 1979.

Freemantle, Anne. *Woman's Way to God.* New York: St. Martin's Press, 1977.

French, Marilyn. *The Woman's Room.* New York: Simon and Schuster, 1977.

Friand, Barbara. "Loneliness and Loving." *Soundings* 49 (1980) pp. 74-79.

Friday, Nancy. *My Mother, My Self*. New York: Delacorte, 1977.

Friedan, Betty. *The Feminine Mystique*. New York: Bantam, 1963.

Fromm, Erich. *The Art of Loving*. New York: Harper & Row, 1956.

Goodman, Ellen. *Turning Points*. New York: Fawcett Columbine, 1977.

Gollwitzer, Helmut. *Song of Love: A Biblical Understanding of Sex*. Philadelphia: Fortress, 1978.

Gould, Carol C. and Marx W. Wartorsky, eds. *Women and Philosophy: Toward a Theory of Liberation*. New York: Putnam and Sons, 1976.

Govaart-Halkes. *Frau, Welt, Kirche*. Utrech: Styria, 1968.

Greeley, Andrew. *Love and Play*. Chicago: Thomas More Press, 1975.

Grelot, Pierre. *Man and Wife in Scripture*. London: Compass, 1964.

Giele, Janet Zollinger. *Women and the Future*. New York: Free Press, 1978.

Harding, M. Esther. *The Way of All Women*. New York: Harper & Row, 1970.

Haring, Bernard, C.Ss.R. *The Christian Existentialist: The Philosophy and Theology of Self-Fulfillment in Modern Society*. New York: New York University Press, 1968.

_____. *Marriage in the Modern World*. Westminster, MD: Newman, 1965.

_____. *The Sacraments in Your Everyday Life*. Liguori, MO: Liguori Publications, 1976.

Harper, Ralph. *Human Love, Existential and Mystical*. Baltimore: Johns Hopkins Press, 1966.

Harrington, Wilfrid J., O.P. *The Promise to Love: A Scriptural View of Marriage*. Staten Island, N.Y.: Alba House, 1968.

Hart, Thomas N. *Living Happily Everafter: Toward a Theology of Marriage (Christian)*. New York: Paulist Press, 1979.

Hassan, Bernard. *The American Catholic Catalog*. San Francisco: Harper & Row, 1980.

Haughton, Rosemary. *Problems of Christian Marriage*. New York: Deus Books, 1968.

_____. *The Theology of Experience*. New York: Newman, 1972.

_____. *The Theology of Marriage*. Hales Corners, WI: Clergy Book Service, 1971.

_____. *Why Be a Christian?* Philadelphia: Lippincott, 1968.

Haughey, John C., S.J. *Should Anyone Say Forever? On Making, Keeping and Breaking Commitments*. Garden City, N.Y.: Doubleday, 1975.

Heilbrun, Carolyn G. *Reinventing Womanhood.* New York: W. W. Norton, 1979.

Hellwig, Monika. *The Meaning of the Sacraments.* Dayton, Ohio: Pflaum Press, 1972.

Horney, Karen, M.D. *Feminine Psychology.* New York: Norton, 1967.

Janeway, Elizabeth. *Powers of the Weak.* New York: Knopf, 1980.

Jewett, Paul K. *Man as Male and Female.* Grand Rapids, MI: Eerdmans, 1975.

Joyce, Gerald P. and James R. Zullo. "Ministry to Marital Growth: A Developmental Perspective." *Chicago Studies.* 18 (1979) pp. 263-278.

Joyce, Mary Rosera and Robert E. Joyce. *New Dynamics in Sexual Love.* Collegeville, MN: St. John's University Press, 1970.

Kasper, Walter. *Theology of Christian Marriage.* New York: Seabury Press, 1980.

Keane, Philip S., S.S. *Sexual Morality: A Catholic Perspective.* New York: Paulist Press, 1977.

Kelleher, Stephen J. *Divorce and Remarriage for Catholics.* Garden City, NY: Doubleday, 1976.

Kelly, George A. *The Catholic Marriage Manual.* New York: Random House, 1958.

Kelsey, Morton T. *Myth, History and Faith.* New York: Paulist Press, 1974.

Kennedy, Eugene C. *In the Spirit, in the Flesh.* Garden City, NY: Doubleday, 1971.

_____. *What a Modern Catholic Believes About Marriage.* Chicago: Thomas More Press, 1972.

Kerken, L. Vander, S.J. *Loneliness and Love.* New York: Sheed and Ward, 1967.

Kindregen, Charles P. *A Theology of Marriage.* Encino, CA: Benziger, 1974.

Kolbenschlag, Madonna. *Kiss Sleeping Beauty Good-Bye.* Garden City, NY: Doubleday, 1979.

Kress, Robert. *Whither Womankind?* St. Meinrad, IN: Abbey Press, 1975.

Kung, Hans. *On Being a Christian.* Garden City, NY: Doubleday, 1974.

_____. *Signposts for the Future.* Garden City, NY: Doubleday, 1978.

Lakoff, Robin. *Language and Woman's Place.* New York: Harper & Row, 1975.

Lasch, Christopher. *The Culture of Narcissism*. New York: Warner, 1979.

———. *Haven in a Heartless World: The Family Besieged*. New York: Basic Books, Inc., 1977.

Lepp, Ignace. *Love Builds Mankind*. Denville, NJ: Dimension Books, 1971.

Leslie, Robert C. *Jesus and Logotherapy*. Nashville, TN: Abingdon, 1952.

Lewis, C. S. *Mere Christianity*. New York: Macmillan, 1952.

Lidz, Theodore. *The Person*. New York: Basic Books, 1968.

Mallett, Harold M. *Keeping Peace in the Family*. Nashville, TN: Abingdon, 1973.

Mandelbaum, Bernard. *Add Life to Your Years*. New York: Grosset and Dunlap, 1973.

Marcel, Gabriel. *Creative Fidelity*. New York: Farrar, Strauss, 1964.

March, W. "Toward a Renewal of the Theology of Marriage." *The Thomist* 30 (1966) pp. 307-342.

Martin, Del. *Battered Wives*. New York: Pocket Books, 1976.

Martin, M. Kay and Barbara Voorhies. *Female of the Species*. New York: Columbia University Press, 1975.

May, Robert. *Sex and Fantasy*. New York: Norton, 1980.

May, Rollo. *Love and Will*. New York: Norton, 1969.

———. *Man's Search for Himself*. New York: Delta, 1953.

———. *Power and Innocence*. New York: Norton, 1972.

Mayerhoff, Milton. *On Caring*. New York: Perennial Library, 1971.

McBride, Angela Barron. *A Married Feminist*. New York: Harper & Row, 1976.

McCready, William C. "Marriage as an Institution of Socialization." *Chicago Studies* 18 (1979) pp. 297-310.

McGrath, S. Albertus Magnus. *What a Modern Catholic Believes About Women*. Chicago: Thomas More Press, 1971.

McLennan, John F. *Primitive Marriage*. Chicago: University of Chicago Press, 1970.

Meyendorf, John. *Marriage: An Orthodox Perspective*. 2nd ed. St. Vladimir's Seminary Press, 1975.

Miller, Casey and Kate Swift. *Words and Women*. Garden City, NY: Doubleday, 1977.

Miller, Jean Baker, M.D. *Toward a New Psychology of Women*. Boston: Beacon Press, 1976.

Mitchell, Juliet. *Women's Estate*. New York: Vintage, 1973.

Moltmann, Jurgen. *Man: Christian Anthropology in the Conflicts of the Present*. Philadelphia: Fortress, 1974.

Monks of Solesmes. *The Woman in the Modern World*. Boston: St. Paul Editions, 1958.

Morgan, Robin. *Sisterhood Is Powerful*. New York: Vintage, 1970.

Mosshamer, Ottilie. *The Priest and Womanhood*. Westminister, MD: Newman, 1964.

Murstein, Bernard. *Love, Sex and Marriage Through the Ages*. New York: Springer, 1974.

Nellis, Muriel. *The Female Fix*. Boston: Houghton-Mifflin, 1980.

Nelson, James R. *Embodiment*. Minneapolis, MN: Augsburg, 1978.

Nilson, John. "The Love at the Center of Love." *Chicago Studies*. 18 (1979) pp. 239-250.

Newland, Kathleen. *The Sisterhood of Man*. New York: Norton, 1979.

Novak, Michael. *All the Catholic People*. New York: Herder and Herder, 1971.

_____. ed. *The Experience of Marriage: The Testimony of Catholic Laymen*. New York: Macmillan, 1964.

_____. *The Experience of Nothingness*. New York: Harper & Row, 1970.

_____. *A Time to Build*. New York: Macmillan, 1964.

Nyberg, Kathleen Neill. *The New Eve*. Nashville, TN: Abingdon, 1967.

Oakley, Ann. *Woman's Work: The Housewife, Past and Present*. New York: Pantheon, 1974.

O'Callaghan, Denis. "Marriage: Institution or Contract?" *The Irish Ecclesiastical Record*. 109 (1968) pp. 265-269.

O'Collins, Gerald. *The Second Journey*. New York: Paulist Press, 1968.

O'Grady, John F. *Christian Anthropology*. New York: Paulist Press, 1976.

O'Neill, Nena and George. *Open Marriage*. New York: Evans, 1972.

Origina. (1979) 9.

Oraison, Marc. *The Human Mystery of Sexuality*. New York: Sheed and Ward, 1967.

_____. *Mand and Wife: The Physical and Spiritual Foundations of Marriage*. New York: Macmillan, 1958.

Osborne, Martha Lee. *Genuine Risk*. Indianapolis: Hackett, 1981.

_____. ed. *Woman in Western Thought*. New York: Random House, 1979.

Padovano, Anthony T. *Belief in Human Life*. Paramus, NJ: Pastoral Education Service, 1969.

Pagels, Elaine. *The Gnostic Gospels*. New York: Random House, 1979.

Palmer, Paul F., S.J. "Christian Marriage: Contract or Covenant." *Theological Studies* 33 (1972) pp. 617-665.

Patai, Raphael. *Family, Love in the Bible*. London: Macgibbin and Kee, 1960.

Paul VI, Pope. *Humanae Vitae*.

Peck, Ellen. *A Funny Thing Happened on the Way to Equality*. Englewood Cliffs, NJ: Prentice-Hall, 1975.

Pieper, Josef. *About Love*. Chicago: Franciscan Herald Press, 1972.

Pincus, Lily and Christopher Dare. *Secrets in the Family*. New York: Harper & Row, 1978.

Pittenger, Norman. "Process Theology: a Whiteheadian Version. *Religious Experience and Process Theology*, edited by Harry James Cargas and Bernard Lee. New York: Paulist Press, 1976.

Poster, Mark. *Critical Theory of the Family*. New York: Continuum, 1980.

Putney, Snell and Gail J. Putney. *The Adjusted American*. New York: Perennial Library, 1964.

Rahner, Karl. *Foundations of Christian Faith*. New York: Seabury Press, 1978.

_____. *Marriage*. Denville, NJ: Dimension Books, 1970.

_____. "Marriage as Sacrament." *Theological Investigations* X. New York: Seabury Press, 1973.

Regan, George M., C.M. *New Trends in Moral Theology*. New York: Newman, 1971.

Rich, Adrienne. *Of Woman Born*. New York: Bantam, 1976.

Ruether, Rosemary Radford. "The Feminist Critique in Religious Studies." *Soundings* 54 (1981) pp. 388-403.

_____. *Liberation Theology*. New York: Paulist Press, 1972.

_____. *New Woman, New Earth*. New York: Seabury Press, 1975.

_____ and Eleanor McLaughlin, eds. *Women of Spirit*. New York: Simon and Schuster, 1979.

Richardson, Herbert. *Toward an American Theology*. New York: Harper & Row, 1967.

Samuel, Dorothy T. *Love, Liberation and Marriage*. New York: Funk and Wagnalls, 1976.

Sanguiliano, Iris. *In Her Time*. New York: Wm. Morrow, 1978.

Scanzoni, John. *Sexual Bargaining*. Englewood Cliffs, NJ: Prentice-Hall, 1970.

Schnell, Maxine. *Limits: A Search for New Values*. New York: Potter, 1981.

Skolnick, Arlene and Jerome. *Family in Transition*. 3rd ed. Boston: Little, Brown, 1980.

Schillebeeckx, Edward. *Marriage: Human Reality and Saving Mystery*. London: Sheed and Ward, 1965.

Siegle, Bernard Andrew. *Marriage Today: A Commentary on the Code of Canon Law*. New York: Alba House, 1979.

Slater, Philip. *Footholds: Understanding the Shifting Sexual and Family Tensions in Our Culture*. Boston: Beacon Press, 1977.

_____. *The Pursuit of Loneliness*. Boston: Beacon Press, 1977.

Span, Paula. "Does it Have to be Lonely at the Top?" Baltimore Magazine, 73 (1980), 5.

Stannard, Una. *Mrs. Man*. San Francisco: Germain Books, 1977.

Stapleton, Jean and Richard Bright. *Equal Marriage*. New York: Harper & Row, 1976.

Steinmetz, Urban. *The Sexual Christian*. St. Meinrad, IN: Abbey Press, 1972.

Strouse, Jean, ed. *Women and Analysis*. New York: Grossman, 1974.

Studia Canonica. (1979) 13, 1.

Thomas, David W. *Family Life in the Church*. New York: Paulist Press, 1979.

Toffler, Alvin. *The Third Wave*. New York: Wm. Morrow, 1980.

Tournier, Paul. *The Meaning of Persons*. New York: Harper & Row, 1957.

_____. *The Violence Within*. New York: Harper & Row, 1978.

"A Vision and Strategy." The Plan of Pastoral Action for Family Ministry. National Conference of Catholic Bishops, United States Catholic Conference, 1978.

Vaillancourt, Raymond. *Toward a Renewal of Sacramental Theology*. Collegeville, MN: Liturgical Press, 1979.

Von Gagern, Frederick, M.D. *New Views on Sex, Marriage, Love*. New York: Paulist Press, 1968.

Wagner, Lenore. *The Battered Woman*. New York: Harper & Row, 1979.

Wahlberg, Rachel Conrad. *Jesus and the Freed Woman*. New York: Paulist Press, 1978.

Walsh, Sister Mary Ann, R.S.M. "Why It's Harder to Get Married in the Church." *U. S. Catholic*. (1980) 45, 6. pp. 31-38.

Whitehead, Alfred North. *Religion in the Making*. New York: New American Library, 1926.

Whitehead, James D. and Evelyn Eaton Whitehead. *Christian Life Patterns*. Garden City, NY: Doubleday, 1979.

_____. "Intimacy and the Christian Family." *New Catholic World*. (1979) 222, 1332. pp. 253-255.

Wills, Gary. *Bare Ruined Choirs*. New York: Delta, 1971.

Wojtyla, Karol. *Love and Responsibility*. New York: Farrar, Strauss and Giroux, 1980.

Wrenn, Lawrence G. *Decisions*. Toledo, OH: Canon Law Society of America, 1980.

Yankelovich, Daniel. *New Rules*. New York: Random House, 1981.